Rules
of Order

Fourth Edition

Geoffrey H. Stanford

M&S

National Library of Canada Cataloguing in Publication

Stanford, G. H. (Geoffrey Hunt), 1906-
Bourinot's Rules of order

4th ed.
Includes index.
ISBN 0-7710-8336-X

1. Canada. Parliament. House of Commons – Rules and practice.   2. Public meetings.   I. Bourinot, John George, Sir, 1837-1902. Bourinot's rules of order.   II. Title.   III. Title: Rules of order.

JL148.B72 1995   328.71'05   C95-930695-1

We acknowledge the financial support of the Government of Canada through the Book Publishing Industry Development Program and that of the Government of Ontario through the Ontario Media Development Corporation's Ontario Book Initiative. We further acknowledge the support of the Canada Council for the Arts and the Ontario Arts Council for our publishing program.

Printed and bound in Canada

McClelland & Stewart Ltd.
The Canadian Publishers
481 University Avenue
Toronto, Ontario
M5G 2E9
www.mcclelland.com

5 6 7   04 03

Contents

Introduction   9

Glossary   13

Part I: The Parliamentary Rules

Article   1. Days and Times   18

               2. Election of Speaker   19

               3. Duties of Speaker   19

               4. Deputy Speaker   20

               5. Officers of the House   20

               6. Attendance and Quorum   21

               7. Order of Business   21

               8. Motions   22

               9. Amendments   23

              10. Debate   24

              11. Dilatory Motions   25

              12. Special Motions   25

              13. Putting the Question   27

              14. Order   28

              15. Privilege   28

              16. Decorum   29

              17. Questions   30

              18. Committees of the Whole House   31

              19. Standing, Special and Legislative
                   Committees   32

              20. Petitions   33

              21. Legislative Process   34

              22. Private Bills   36

              23. Private Members' Bills   37

              24. Reports   38

Part II: Rules and Usages for Assemblies Generally

Article   25. Rules   39
26. Changing the Rules   40
27. Suspension of Rules   40
28. Assemblies   40
29. Notice of Meetings   41
30. The Presiding Officer   42
31. Absence of Presiding Officer   42
32. Duties of the Chair   43
33. Choosing the Presiding Officer   44
34. Quorum   45
35. Order of Business   46
36. Motions   46
37. Reconsideration   48
38. Amendments   48
39. Notice of Motion   49
40. Motions for Special Purposes   50
41. Debate   52
42. Putting the Question   53
43. Methods of Voting   54
44. Order   56
45. Privilege   57
46. Closing the Meeting   57
47. Minutes and Records   58
48. Committees   60
49. Reports   61
50. General   62

Part III: Assemblies and Organizations

Article   51. Lawful and Unlawful Assemblies   64
52. Procedure at Public Meetings   65
53. Formation of Associations, Societies, etc.   67
54. Draft Constitution   70
55. Election of Officers   72

	56. Incorporation	75
	57. Winding Up	76
	58. Meetings for Special Purposes	77

Part IV: Company Meetings

Article	59. General	81
	60. By-Laws	83
	61. Directors	83
	62. Meetings of Directors	86
	63. Shareholders' Meetings	87
	64. Minutes	92
	65. Company Books and Records	93

Part V: Some Illustrations

Suspension of Rules	95
Minutes	95
Report of Committee	96
Electing a Chair of a Meeting Called for a Special Purpose	97
Electing a Chair of a Formative Meeting	98
Choosing a Chair in the Absence of Regular Presiding Officers	98
Quorum	98
Motions	99
Postponement of Action on Motion	100
Notice of Motion	102
Order	102
Privilege	103
Form of Minutes	104
Form of Report	106
Form of Minutes for Board of Directors	106
Form of Minutes for Shareholders' Meeting	107

Index	110

Introduction

People attending a formal meeting for the first time are often mystified – even intimidated – by the rules of order used. With their motions and seconders and calls for "the previous question" the rules seem devised to complicate decision making. But anyone who has ever attended a large meeting that tried to make its decisions through consensus, without rules of procedure, will appreciate that a few rules would have made the process less protracted and repetitive.

Parliamentary rules of order, in one version or another, are used around the world for meetings of all kinds because they are fair and democratic, allowing for decisions to be made on the basis of the will of the majority, while respecting the opinions of the minority and permitting all participants to express their views without fear of censure. *Bourinot's Rules of Order* is based on the parliamentary rules of the House of Commons in Ottawa.

The origins of these rules date back to the signing of the Magna Carta in Britain in 1215, which was the first attempt to place constitutional limits on the power of the monarchy. The rules developed over the centuries, reflecting parliament's growing independence and its increasing commitment to democratic practice. The British Empire brought parliamentary rules to all parts of the globe, and even colonies that rebelled against Britain, such as the American colonies, continued to use these rules, modifying the details for their own legislative purposes. Parliamentary rules were used in Canada long before Confederation, but the Constitution Act of 1867 confirmed them as the rules of order for the Canadian Parliament.

The underlying objective of parliamentary procedure is to establish and maintain conditions in the House of Commons that permit a free and fair exchange of views on issues brought to the members for a decision. As members of Parliament represent different parties and local interests, and often come from different cultural backgrounds, the rules have to be precise and fair and must be even-handedly applied by a Speaker or other presiding officer whose impartiality and understanding of their purpose is beyond question.

Jeremy Bentham (1748–1832), an English political theorist, set out in his "Essay on Political Tactics" what he considered to be the four fundamental rules or principles for legislative procedures. The ideas of Bentham and his followers were influential in the reform of the British parliament in the nineteenth century.

Publicity, says Bentham, is the most important of these principles. All proceedings of a parliament should be open to public scrutiny, and the members of the parliament, the press, and through them the public, should receive adequate notice of the hours of sitting and of the business that will be considered at any sitting. Only by means of such publicity could the populace give its support and assent to the formulation of new laws.

Bentham's second principle concerns the absolute impartiality of the Speaker or presiding officer. He recommends that there is only one presiding officer, but that a substitute should be available at all times. He goes on to say that the Speaker performs the two functions of being a judge between individual members, and of being an agent of the whole assembly. To preserve impartiality, the Speaker should be excluded from usual parliamentary activity and lose his (or her) rights as a member to propose motions, to participate in debate, or to vote. The Speaker cannot be a judge unless he (or she) is above all suspicion of partisanship, and the Speaker's actions, in turn, must be subject to the final authority of the assembly.

The third principle concerns the forms of parliamentary procedure. Bentham suggests that proposition, debate, and voting be conducted in separate stages. This provides for orderly progress and avoids a confusion of issues.

Bentham's final principle has to do with freedom of speech. He contends that members should be allowed to speak as often as they wish, to prevent the minority from being overwhelmed. Most modern legislatures find themselves unable to comply with this dictum; their rules of procedure as set out in Standing Orders usually ensure a fair allocation of time for the expression of opinion, but place certain limits on how that time is used, or on how long each member can speak, so that decisions can be made and the subordination of parliamentary rights to an individual or minority is avoided.

Parliament, the model for all assemblies, should be, in the words of Winston Churchill, "a strong, easy, flexible instrument of free debate." It achieves this by observing sensible rules that allow the orderly consideration of the questions before it, leading to a decision that expresses the House's collective will or opinion. Unanimity cannot always be reached, but procedures that ensure proper deliberation of an issue will lead to acceptance and wider support of the outcome and will also help to avoid misunderstandings and friction in the process. In effect, good procedure is fair play and common sense built on a solid foundation of acknowledged principle. Above all, the rules must not change in the middle of the game.

Bourinot's Rules of Order was originally written by Sir John George Bourinot, Chief Clerk of the House of Commons from 1880 until his death in 1902, so that Canadians might better understand the procedures of the House of Commons. The second edition, published in 1962, incorporated the many revisions to the Standing Orders of House of Commons that had modified the original rules and introduced adaptations of the rules for use by other assemblies, including shareholders' meetings. The third edition, published in 1977, again brought the rules up to date and simplified both the concepts and the language used to describe them. It also expanded the information given on the use of these rules by non-parliamentary assemblies.

This fourth edition continues this custom. It incorporates the substantive revisions made to the Standing Orders of the House of Commons and to the federal legislation governing corporations, the Canada

Business Corporations Act, since the last edition of *Bourinot's Rules of Order* was published. It also attempts, in its choice of language, both to recognize the increasingly equal role of men and women in public life and to express the rules in plainer English. It follows the book's original objective and format: procedures in the House of Commons are described in the first chapter, and subsequent chapters detail how an adaptation of these procedures can be used by other assemblies and organizations.

For their invaluable help in the preparation of this edition, the publishers would like especially to thank N. William Ross and Wayne T. Egan of Weir & Foulds, Barristers & Solicitors.

Glossary

Abstention The refusal to vote either for or against a motion. Under parliamentary rules, abstentions do not have to be noted in the official record of a vote.

Acclamation When only one candidate comes forward for election to any office, he or she is said to be elected or returned to that office by acclamation.

Adjourn To suspend proceedings to another time and/or place.

Agenda Literally, this means the things to be done. It is a list of the items to be dealt with at a meeting, usually arranged in the order in which they will be addressed.

Amendment An alteration of a main motion by substituting, adding or deleting a word or words without materially altering the basic intent of the main motion. An amendment must be proposed by motion and must be seconded. Amendments can offer alternatives to the motion being considered, but cannot be hostile to its intent.

Ballot The paper on which a voter indicates his or her choice by marking an X against the name or other representation of a candidate in an election or against a question of opinion in a referendum.

By-laws The rules or directives that govern the internal affairs of an organization.

Casting Vote A single vote (usually the prerogative of the chair) that determines an issue when a vote on the motion has resulted in a tie.

Closure An action that brings debate on an issue to a conclusion by a specified time, thus forcing a decision on that issue at that time. In the House of Commons, it is a procedure that forbids any further adjournment of debate and requires that the motion is voted on by the end of the current sitting.

Committee of the Whole The entire body of an assembly, including the House of Commons, meeting as a committee under a chair other than the Speaker or regular chair. Its purpose is to facilitate discussion by using less strict rules than those used in a formal meeting of the assembly.

Constitution The fundamental laws and principles that establish an institution and set out its nature, functions and limits.

Division The separation for the purpose of voting of those who support and those who oppose a motion. Each member's vote is recorded as his or her name is called from the membership roll.

Ex Officio By virtue of office or position.

Majority More than half of the total number of the membership of an organization or of members present at a regularly constituted meeting with a quorum in attendance.

Motions (a) A substantive, or main, motion is a formal proposal placed before a meeting by one member, the mover of the motion, for debate and a decision, usually taken by vote. Most, but not all, motions must be supported by a second member, the seconder, before they can be debated and decided.

(b) A subsidiary motion is one that delays or defers a decision on a main motion or brings it to an immediate vote, such as the motion for the previous question.

(c) Dilatory motions have the effect of postponing consideration of a question for the time being, e.g., motions for reading the orders of the day, for proceeding to another order of business, for the adjournment of the House or the debate.

Mover A person who presents or proposes a motion or an amendment.

Officer A person elected to a position of authority, called an office, within an organization. Officers usually are the president, vice-president, treasurer and secretary. Together they can also act as a management or executive committee.

Order (a) Behaviour in a meeting which permits members to conduct its business without disruption.

(b) An admonition (call to order) by the Speaker or chair to stop any disruption of the meeting by a participant or participants.

(c) An issue (point of order) raised by a participant at a meeting claiming that the procedures of the meeting or of an individual participant are contrary to procedural rules or practices.

Order Paper The parliamentary equivalent of an agenda. A list of the things to be done or the business to be transacted in the day's proceedings.

Orders of the Day The items constituting the Order Paper of the House of Commons.

Plurality In a contest between three or more candidates for office, the plurality is the majority vote received by the winning candidate, when the votes for that person are less than half the number of votes cast. (See Majority.)

Privilege Privilege is the rights and immunities of members of Parliament, both as individuals and collectively as the House of Commons. In non-parliamentary bodies, privilege is often regarded as the members' right to correct inaccuracies or explain circumstances they believe affect themselves adversely or reflect improperly upon the organization as a whole. The question of whether a matter is properly one of privilege is determined by the Speaker or chair.

Pro Tem. For the time being.

Question The issue before a meeting on which a decision has to be made. A question cannot be debated, amended or voted on until it has been proposed as a motion. To "put the question" ends debate and submits the motion to a vote.

Quorum The number of people required to be present at a meeting to validate the transaction of its business.

Refer To send an issue to a committee for study and report before the main body makes its decision on the issue.

Resolution A proposal or motion that declares the *opinion* of an organization rather than its intent to act on a certain matter.

Scrutineer A person appointed to examine and verify the admissibility of the ballots cast in any voting procedure. The scrutineer can also be assigned the function of teller. In company meetings, his or her duties may include the determination of the number of shareholders present in person or by proxy and, for voting purposes, the number of shares each represents.

Seconder A person who formally supports a motion or amendment at the time it is proposed.

Supply In parliamentary terminology, "supply" or "appropriation" refers to the moneys requested by the government for its various purposes. Part of the business of supply is dealt with by the House convened as a committee of the whole.

Table To place a document before a meeting for its consideration or consultation.

Teller A person appointed to count votes.

Two-Thirds Vote A requirement that a motion passes only if two-thirds or more of the votes support it. This requirement is usually applied only to major issues being put to the vote, such as a motion to reconsider.

Unparliamentary Language Words or expressions that violate the proprieties of the House of Commons or the Senate.

Ways and Means In Parliament, the term "ways and means" refers to the moneys the government requires for its various purposes. The business of ways and means has two major elements: the presentation of the budget and the introduction of tax bills.

PART I

The Parliamentary Rules

Procedure in the Canadian House of Commons is governed by the Standing Orders of the House, which are published under the authority of the Speaker by the Canada Communications Group. The Standing Orders set out formally and officially all of the conditions under which the House functions and state rules that cover all of the circumstances likely to be encountered in conducting the business of the House. They constitute the basis of the Speaker's administration of parliamentary affairs and are his or her reference in making rulings that affect the day-to-day conduct of debate. It is the duty of all new members to familiarize themselves with the Standing Orders and to conduct themselves accordingly.

A comprehensive outline of the Standing Orders would serve little useful purpose in this book, but because they delineate the rules of procedure for every other type of formal assembly, both public and private, a review of their main provisions is pertinent.

1. Days and Times
The days and times of the sittings of the House of Commons while it is in session are set out in the Standing Orders, as are the daily routine, the order of the business to be considered, and the rules that must be followed by a member seeking any variation in normal procedure. This information is necessary to permit the members, who come from all

parts of the country, to organize their arrangements for attendance. The actual convening of a Parliament is the prerogative of the Crown, acting on the advice of the government, which must have the support of the majority of the House of Commons to proceed.

2. Election of Speaker

Section 44 of the Constitution Act of 1867 directs the House of Commons at its first assembly after a general election to elect one of its members to be the Speaker of the House. Since 1986 the Speaker has been elected by a secret ballot conducted under the auspices of a temporary chairman,[*] who is the member with the longest unbroken period of service and who is neither in the cabinet nor holds any office in the House. All eligible members, with the exception of ministers of the Crown, party leaders, and those who have indicated they do not wish to be considered, are candidates for this office. The members vote by writing the name of their choice on a ballot. After this and all subsequent rounds of voting, the names of members who received less than five per cent of the vote, and of the member receiving the least number of votes, are dropped. Voting continues until one member receives a majority of the votes cast.

3. Duties of Speaker

The Speaker presides at all meetings of the House of Commons, but does not participate in debate and has no vote except when there has been a tie vote (an equal number of votes for and against) among the members. It is the Speaker's duty to preserve order and decorum and to decide all questions of order, citing the applicable Standing Order or other authority. The Speaker's decision is not subject to appeal. Any question of privilege (see Article 15) raised by a member is taken into consideration by the Speaker either immediately or at a time he or she determines.

A member who wishes to speak while in the House must rise in his or her place (i.e., his or her assigned seat) and wait to be recognized by the Speaker. Should the member be called to order by the Speaker at

---

[*] In accordance with the language used in the House of Commons, the term chairman is used throughout this chapter.

any time, he or she must sit down until the breach of order is dealt with. Any member who persists in irrelevance or repetition, or in using unparliamentary language, may be directed by the Speaker to discontinue the speech. Persistent failure to comply with the Speaker's orders may result in a member's suspension from the House.

The Speaker is the judge of the propriety of any motion made in the House. Both prior to and at the conclusion of debate on any substantive motion, the Speaker reads, or has read, the terms of the motion in both official languages. At the conclusion of the debate, the Speaker puts the question to the House, asking whether members wish to adopt the motion, and takes the sense of the meeting in either a voice or a recorded vote.

4. Deputy Speaker

A Deputy Speaker is also chosen at the start of each new Parliament to assume all the duties of the Speaker in the latter's absence. The Standing Orders do not set out the terms of the Deputy Speaker's election. By custom, however, the prime minister moves that the House appoint a certain member – usually a government member – as chairman of committees of the whole House, who acts as Deputy Speaker. A deputy chairman of committees of the whole and an assistant deputy chairman are appointed in the same way, but serve only for a single session, not for an entire Parliament. When the Speaker is absent from the House of Commons, the Deputy Speaker, the deputy chairman or the assistant deputy chairman takes the chair.

5. Officers of the House

The Clerk of the House is the chief procedural adviser to the Speaker and to members of Parliament. The Clerk is also responsible for all aspects of the administration of the House of Commons and is secretary to the Board of Internal Economy, the body set up by legislation to oversee the administration of the House. As well, the Clerk is responsible for the safekeeping of all the papers and records of the House and supervises the other parliamentary clerks and officers under the general authority of the Speaker and the House as a whole. The Clerk provides the Speaker each day with the written order of business for that day, called the Order Paper, and among other duties ensures the availability of the legal and other services required by the House.

When the Speaker has read or proposed a motion to the House, the Clerk makes a record of it in the journal, but takes no note of members' speeches.

The Deputy Clerk seconds the Clerk in his or her functions and is responsible for the Administration Services of the House of Commons.

The Sergeant-at-Arms is responsible for security within the Parliamentary precincts. He or she has charge of the Mace, the symbol of parliamentary authority, and performs various ceremonial functions.

6. Attendance and Quorum

Every member must attend the sittings of the House unless he or she is unable to attend because of other parliamentary activities or public or official business. Full attendance is rarely achieved, but penalties are imposed when a member's absence is unduly prolonged. At least twenty members must be present, including the Speaker, to permit the House to exercise its powers; this number constitutes a quorum. If at the time of meeting there is no quorum present, the Speaker adjourns the House until the next sitting day and directs the Clerk to record the time of adjournment and the names of the members present.

Should the House be suddenly adjourned due to the loss of quorum, any question under consideration keeps its place on the Order Paper for the next sitting, unless it is an item of private members' business not selected to be put to a vote (see Article 23), in which case, the question is dropped from the Order Paper.

A quorum of any committee of the whole is also twenty. A quorum of a standing or special committee is a majority of the members, unless otherwise specifically stated.

7. Order of Business

The order of the business to be dealt with by the House each day is set out in the Standing Orders. This allows members with duties outside the House to be aware of the business being transacted in the House each day. Members must be notified in advance of any alteration made to this order.

A motion for reading the Orders of the Day has to be decided immediately, ahead of any other motion before the House.

8. Motions

A question to be considered by the House is presented as a motion, moved by one member and seconded by another. Forty-eight hours' notice must be given of most substantive motions. The Speaker proposes the motion to the House by reading it, or having it read, in both French and English, at which point it is formally entered in the records. It is then subject to debate. After debate, the motion may be accepted, amended or rejected by the House.

When a motion in either its original or amended form is adopted it becomes either a resolution, through which the House declares its opinion or purpose, or an order, through which the House directs its members, committees, officers and proceedings. Procedures governing the making, debate and disposition of motions are laid down in the Standing Orders. A motion once made may be withdrawn by the mover, but only with the *unanimous* consent of the House.

To avoid misunderstandings and encourage informed debate, any member may require that the question under consideration be read at any time during the debate, but not so as to interrupt the member speaking.

Once a motion is defeated it cannot be reintroduced except in the form of a new proposal that is sufficiently different in its terms as to constitute a different question. The Speaker rules on the acceptability of any new motion.

When a question is under consideration no other substantive motion may be made, but there are a number of so-called privileged motions that are acceptable, e.g., to amend, to adjourn, to take various actions designed to delay resolution of the issue or to bring debate to a conclusion.

Once adopted, a motion cannot be debated further except for the purpose of moving that it be rescinded. In such a case a member may, after due notice, move "That the order or resolution of the House that is recorded in the 'Journals' of (date) at page (number) and which reads (text of resolution) be rescinded."

9. Amendments

While a substantive motion is under debate any member may, without notice, move a motion to amend it. An amendment is designed to alter or vary the terms of the main motion without substantially changing its intent; it may propose that certain words be omitted altogether, that they be replaced by others, or that other words be inserted or added. Every amendment must be strictly relevant to the question being considered. An amendment that would simply counter the intent of the main motion is not acceptable. Once a motion to amend has been moved and seconded, the main motion is set aside until the amendment has been decided.

Any member may move to amend the amendment itself, but such a subamendment can modify only the amendment; it cannot directly modify the main motion. Just as an amendment must be relevant to the main motion, a subamendment must be relevant to the amendment.

Any subamendment and amendment must be resolved before a new amendment to the main motion can be entertained. There is, however, no limit to the number of amendments and subamendments that may be proposed.

After an amendment to a motion has been moved and seconded, the Speaker restates the original motion, naming its mover and seconder, and the amendment and its mover and seconder, before asking if it is the "pleasure of the House to adopt the said amendment."

As far as it is practical, debate is confined to the proposed amendment. If the amendment is defeated, the Speaker will again state the main motion, which may be debated or another amendment may be offered. If the amendment is adopted, the Speaker will ask "Is it the pleasure of the House to adopt the main motion (or question) as amended?" The vote at this point may decide the issue, or a member may propose another amendment.

When there are a main motion, an amendment and a subamendment, the Speaker will submit the three motions to the House in reverse order to which they were made, following a procedure similar to the one outlined above.

10. Debate

A member wishing to speak must rise to catch the Speaker's attention. If two or more members rise, the Speaker decides who speaks first, usually calling upon the one who rose first. If the House disagrees with the Speaker's decision, a motion may be made that another member who has risen "be now heard" or "do now speak." This motion is not debatable and must be voted upon at once.

The first to speak in any debate is the member who gave notice of the bill or motion to be considered. When that item is reached on the Order Paper, the Speaker calls on the member by the name of his or her constituency, or by title if the member is a government minister, to indicate whether he or she wishes to proceed. If the member so indicates (by nodding), the Speaker checks that there is a seconder for the motion and then calls upon the first member to move the motion. The member who seconds the motion has the option of speaking to the motion following the mover, but usually waits until later in the debate.

After the opening speech, the Speaker ordinarily recognizes members on either side of the House alternately based on party membership in the House to distribute the time equitably among the various areas of opinion. No other member is allowed to pass between the member who is speaking and the chair, nor to interrupt except to raise a point of order. The debate on most motions is limited under the Standing Orders to either ten or twenty minutes each speaker, except for the member who moves the motion, depending upon the type of debate, e.g., second or third reading of a bill or private members' business.

A member speaking for or against the motion must not read from a prepared text, but may refer to notes. If a member is called to order either by the Speaker or on a point of order raised by another member, he or she sits down while the point is stated. The member can then explain, and the point of order may be debated, but the debate must be strictly relevant to the point of order. The Speaker then rules on the point.

No member may speak twice to a question except to explain a material part of his or her speech which may have been misquoted or misunderstood. The mover of a substantive motion is, however, allowed a reply at the conclusion of the debate. The Speaker informs the House that the mover's reply closes the debate.

Not all motions are debatable. Which are and which are not are clearly set out in the Standing Orders. As a rough guide, substantive issues on which there will obviously be varying opinions are open to debate, while those of a procedural nature are not.

The Speaker does not take part in any debate before the House.

11. Dilatory Motions

There is a class of motions, called dilatory motions, which may be used to avoid dealing with a question for the time being or permanently. They have the effect of delaying or superseding the consideration of a question, and they must be decided immediately without debate or amendment. Dilatory motions include those to postpone consideration of the question to a specified date, to read the Orders of the Day, to proceed to another order, to adjourn the debate, or to adjourn the House.

12. Special Motions

A simple motion to adjourn the House is different from a motion to adjourn the House that is moved for the purpose of discussing a specific matter of urgent public importance. In the latter case, a member must inform the Speaker in writing of what urgent matter he or she wishes to raise one hour prior to seeking leave to move the adjournment of the House. The Speaker then determines, without debate, whether the matter warrants the immediate consideration of the House. In making this decision, the Speaker may consider the expressed wish of the members of the House to debate the matter. The Speaker must be satisfied that it relates to a genuine emergency calling for immediate and urgent consideration, that it does not anticipate future regular business nor revive discussion of issues already dealt with, and that it does not raise a question of privilege. These safeguards are imposed to provide against misuse of the procedure and to ensure that it is used to achieve a definite and acceptable end.

If the Speaker decides that the motion to adjourn the House is acceptable, the emergency debate usually takes place at 8:00 p.m. that day; on Fridays it is dealt with immediately. If debate continues past the normal time of adjournment, the Speaker at the conclusion of the debate or at midnight (4:00 p.m. on Fridays) declares the motion to adjourn to have carried. The motion to adjourn the House to allow discussion of an urgent matter may be withdrawn by the mover with the consent of the House.

A second type of special motion is the "previous question." The object of this motion is to force a vote on the main question. The member wishing to call the question moves "That the question be now put." The motion requires a seconder, but it cannot be moved or seconded by a member who has spoken on the main motion. It can be debated but it cannot be amended. If the motion is agreed to, the House proceeds immediately to vote on the main motion. If defeated, the continuation of the debate is deferred to another day. The "previous question" may be used as a dilatory motion to avoid coming to a decision on a subject under discussion, although this end can be better achieved by moving "That the House proceed to the next order of business," which is a motion that must be voted upon immediately without debate.

A main motion and the previous question may both be superseded by a motion to adjourn the House or to proceed to another order of business. Both of these motions must be decided at once without amendment or debate. If the House adjourns at the specified hour without the question being put to a vote, a motion for the previous question does not lapse. The debate may be carried over from day to day.

The most decisive action to terminate debate is closure. Having given notice to the House at least twenty-four hours earlier, a minister may, immediately before an adjourned debate is to be resumed, move that the debate shall not be further adjourned. Only a minister may move such a motion, and he or she must give at least twenty-four hours' notice to the House to allow all interested members to attend the debate. A closure motion must be decided without debate or amendment. If the motion carries, during the ensuing debate on the main motion no member may speak for longer than twenty minutes and no member who has already spoken may speak again except to an amendment or subamendment. The question must be decided by the conclusion of that day's sitting, and no member is allowed to rise to speak after 11:00 p.m.

13. Putting the Question

Debate on a question ends when all members who wish to speak have spoken, or it may be ended by the Speaker under the provisions of a Standing Order or an order of the House. The Speaker then puts the question by reading the motion and asking the House to voice its opinion. The Speaker asks those members in favour of the motion to say "yea" and next asks those members opposed to the motion to say "nay." On the evidence of the voices the Speaker will then declare the motion carried or lost.

If five or more members of the House do not agree with the Speaker's judgement a recorded division may be held, a process that originally entailed the physical separation of those for and against. Now, when the members have each been called in for a recorded division, the Speaker again puts the question and asks those in favour of the motion to rise. As each member stands, a Clerk-at-the-Table (Table Officer) calls out the member's name and the another clerk places a mark against the name on a list of all members. A similar procedure then follows for those opposed to the motion. The clerk counts the votes on both sides and reports the result to the Speaker, who then declares the motion either carried or lost.

In case of a tie vote the Speaker has a casting vote. The Speaker's vote is not an expression of opinion on the merits of the question. According to tradition, the Speaker maintains impartiality by voting only in a way that provides a further opportunity to consider the question, and his or her reasons are recorded.

Members may not enter, leave or cross the House when the Speaker is putting a question. Members who are not present when the question is put cannot vote. While members are expected to vote in every case, there is nothing to oblige them to do so. Any member who inadvertently votes the wrong way cannot correct the mistake except with the unanimous consent of the House. There can be no debate on a question after it has been put by the Speaker.

14. Order

It is the right and duty of every member to bring to the Speaker's attention any deviation or departure from the rules or ordinary procedure of the House during a debate, and any such point of order must be clearly and succinctly stated. When the Speaker or any other member rises on a point of order, the member who has the floor must sit down until the matter is dealt with. A point of order must be raised at the time the alleged irregularity occurs; it is not acceptable if other proceedings have intervened.

The Speaker may permit debate on a question of order before giving a decision, but the debate must be strictly relevant to the point. When the Speaker thinks that there has been an adequate expression of opinion he or she terminates debate and gives a ruling on the point of order, citing the Standing Order or other authority on which the ruling is based. No debate is allowed on the ruling, and the Speaker's decision cannot be appealed.

Sometimes a member will rise on a so-called point of order to refute or dispute a statement by a member who has the floor. The Speaker will simply inform him or her that this is not a point of order and the debate proceeds.

15. Privilege

Parliamentary privilege is the rights that the House collectively and members individually hold that ensure Parliament's ability to function freely. Questions of privilege cover a wide range, but in general they have to do with matters affecting the members' right to sit in the House, freedom of speech while in the House, and contempt of Parliament as a whole. A breach of privilege is, in effect, a wilful disregard by a member or any other person of the freedom, dignity and lawful authority of Parliament.

A question of privilege should be raised as soon as possible after the breach has occurred. If the breach occurred during the normal proceedings of the House, the question must be raised immediately. If it occurred outside the House, one hour's written notice of the question must be given to the Speaker before it is raised in the House.

After hearing the evidence from the member or members involved, the Speaker decides only whether there is prima facie a case of privilege, i.e., whether the evidence warrants the question being given immediate consideration. If the Speaker determines the matter is not prima facie a breach of privilege, he or she may still acknowledge that the complaint is a legitimate grievance. If the Speaker determines that there has been prima facie a breach of privilege, a motion, which usually refers the matter to the Standing Committee on Procedure and House Affairs, is moved. Debate on the motion is given priority. If the House carries the motion, the Standing Committee examines the evidence and may call witnesses, and subsequently reports its findings to the House. A motion that the House concurs in the Standing Committee's findings and recommendations may then be moved.

If the Speaker rules that a question of privilege concerning a member's conduct, election or right to hold a seat is in order, due notice is given to the member so that he or she may be present in the House to reply to the charge. At the start of debate on the motion, the member is permitted to make a statement and then withdraws until the matter is dealt with.

Not infrequently members rise on so-called questions of privilege to correct reports of their speeches or to comment on allegedly inaccurate statements in the news media, but these properly are personal complaints, not matters of privilege, and the Speaker so rules.

16. Decorum

It is the Speaker's duty to preserve order and decorum in the House and to deal promptly and fairly with any breach of order. In doing so, the Speaker states the Standing Order or other authority applicable to the case. No debate is permitted on the Speaker's decision, nor can the decision be appealed to the House. A member called to order for breach of parliamentary decorum is expected to comply at once with any directive given by the Speaker, withdrawing any offensive words or apologizing for any inadvertent infringement of the rules and customs of the House. If the member does not do so and continues with offensive, irrelevant or repetitious remarks despite several warnings from the Speaker to desist, the Speaker may "name" the member for disregarding the authority of the chair. When the member is named, the Speaker can order him or her to withdraw from the Chamber for the rest of the day's sitting (or, in extreme cases, allow the House to take disciplinary action). In the latter case, another member, usually the Government House Leader, proposes a motion to suspend the member from the House for a specified period. This motion cannot be debated or amended. If the motion carries, the member may not enter the Chamber nor serve on parliamentary committees for the duration of the suspension.

17. Questions

Questions that seek information from ministers on matters of urgent public concern, that call a minister to account for the government's actions, or, less commonly, that request information from other members relating to matters connected with the business of the House, may be raised orally in the House during the forty-five-minute Question Period, which is televised. In asking and answering questions no argument or opinion can be offered, and any facts stated must be relevant to the question. A question must not contain charges which the questioner is not prepared to substantiate, must not seek solutions to hypothetical cases and must not seek information from a minister on any matter unconnected to the minister's current portfolio. A question cannot be made the pretext for a debate, and when a question has been fully answered it cannot be renewed.

Both questions and answers must be concise, and no debate is permitted. The minister being interrogated may reply at once, or defer the answer, or take the question as notice, or remain silent. Supplementary questions must contain no preamble and be precise. In recent years, Question Period has become the premier vehicle used by members to ask questions of the government regarding its performance and decisions.

Written questions may also be placed on the Order Paper, but no member may have more than four questions on the Order Paper at any time. A member may also request an oral answer to a question placed on the Order Paper. Written questions are answered by tabling the answers, which are normally printed as if read, or by reading out the answer where an oral reply was requested.

18. Committees of the Whole House

A committee of the whole House is composed of the entire membership of the House. Appropriation bills, or supply bills, which are bills to authorize government expenditures, are referred to a committee of the whole after their second reading. The House may on occasion also send other bills to a committee of the whole instead of to a standing or other committee. Other questions may be referred to committees of the whole when it is desirable to permit freer and fuller consideration than would be possible in a formal sitting of the House.

A member is elected at the start of every Parliament to serve as Deputy Speaker and chairman of committees of the whole. The House also appoints a deputy chairman and assistant deputy chairman to preside in the absence of the Deputy Speaker while the House is in committee of the whole. The chairman maintains order, deciding all questions of order subject to an appeal to the Speaker, but disorder in a committee must be reported to and dealt with by the House itself.

As far as they are applicable, the Standing Orders of the House are observed in committees of the whole, the exceptions being that motions are not seconded, members may speak more than once to the same question, and no member may speak for longer than twenty minutes. Speeches must be strictly relevant to the issue under consideration, and the committee may deal only with matters referred to it. The committee is not at liberty to go beyond its terms of reference.

In committees of the whole, debate is carried on as in the House itself, and a majority decision rules. In the case of a tie vote, the chairman has a casting vote. If a division is required, the votes on each side are counted and reported to the chairman, who declares the motion carried or lost, but names are not recorded.

When the matters referred to a committee of the whole have been fully dealt with, the chairman is directed to report the outcome to the House. Until that is done, the House may not refer to the question or to the committee's deliberations. Whenever a resolution of a committee of the whole is reported to the House, a motion to concur in it must be proposed and decided without debate or amendment.

A committee of the whole may consider a matter in part and report progress to the House, and continue its work when the order for the committee is again read. A motion to "report progress and ask leave to sit again" is equivalent to a motion to adjourn debate and may be used merely to defer discussion.

Should a member wish to have a question entirely set aside, he or she may move that the chairman leave the chair. This motion is always in order, takes precedence over any other motion, and is not debatable. If the majority of members vote for the motion, the chairman at once leaves the chair and, as no report can be made to the House, the bill or question disappears from the Order Paper. It can be restored only by a motion made in the House after due notice.

19. Standing, Special and Legislative Committees

Committees are established to facilitate the conduct of the business of the House and are given different powers according to the tasks assigned them by the House. At the beginning of each session fourteen members are appointed to the Standing Committee on Procedure and House Affairs. This committee acts as a striking committee to prepare and report lists of members to compose the standing committees. There are currently nineteen standing committees, including the Standing Committee on Procedure and House Affairs. They include committees on foreign affairs and international trade; fisheries and oceans; health; industry; justice and legal affairs. There are also three joint standing committees between the House of Commons and the Senate.

The striking committee reports to the House within the first ten sitting days after its appointment or after the start of a new session. After the House concurs in the report, the standing committees continue from session to session within a Parliament, with adjustments in membership as required from time to time.

Standing committees have the power to examine and enquire into all matters referred to them by the House and to report from time to time. Any recommendations and opinions that dissent from the committee's report or are supplementary to it can be stated in an appendix. Unless otherwise ordered by the House, standing committees may send for papers and records, sit while the House is sitting or while it stands adjourned, publish papers and records, summon witnesses, create subcommittees and delegate to them any or all of the committee's powers except the power to report directly to the House.

The House may also from time to time appoint special committees of not more than fifteen members to study specific matters. Each special committee is established by a motion, called an order of reference, that sets out its terms and mandate.

At the start of each session, the Speaker appoints up to twelve members, and thereafter additional members as necessary, to act as chairmen of legislative committees. The Standing Committee on Procedure and House Affairs appoints not more than fifteen members to each legislative committee established by order of the House. The legislative committees examine bills referred to them after second reading.

Each standing or special committee elects its own chairman and two vice-chairmen, who, while in the chair, maintain order and decide all questions of order subject to an appeal to the committee. Disorder in a committee, however, can be censured only by the House on receiving a report of the incident. The Standing Orders of the House must be observed insofar as they are applicable, except orders relating to the seconding of motions, limits on the number of times a member can speak and limits on the length of speeches.

A majority of the members of a committee constitutes a quorum, and a quorum is required whenever a vote, resolution or other decision is taken. A member of the House who is not a member of the committee may nevertheless take part in its public proceedings, but cannot be counted as part of a quorum or vote or move any motion.

20. Petitions

A petition is a written request by members of the public for the House to take action on a particular problem. A petition is sent to a member of Parliament, who, before presenting it, must first submit it to the Clerk of Petitions for certification. All petitions must be addressed to the House of Commons, be within its jurisdiction, be written in temperate language, have the subject matter indicated on every sheet and be signed by at least twenty-five people. Petitions must be written, typewritten or printed on standard-size paper and contain only original signatures and addresses. If all the requisite conditions are met, the Clerk attaches a certificate to that effect to the petition.

The presenting member must endorse, but not sign, the petition before bringing it to the House. Only a member may present a petition, and is held answerable for it by the House. Members may choose not to present a petition. A petition to the House may be presented on behalf of constituents orally by a member during a daily period following the Speaker's call for "Presenting Petitions." This period must last not longer than fifteen minutes. A petition may also be tabled by filing it with the Clerk of the House at any time while the House is sitting.

There is no debate in the House concerning a petition, but the Clerk records its presentation and then sends it to the Privy Council Office, which directs it to the appropriate government department or agency for response. The response must be tabled in the House and sent to the presenting member within forty-five days of the petition's presentation.

21. Legislative Process

Bills may originate in either the House of Commons or the Senate, but any bill involving an expenditure of public money or the imposition of any taxation must be initiated in the House. Public bills may be sponsored either by the government or by a private member. However, only cabinet ministers can introduce Supply (appropriation) or Ways and Means (taxation) bills. Public bills deal with matters of public policy or matters that affect the public interest; they are distinguished from private bills (see Article 22, below).

Every bill to be introduced in the House is listed on the Order Paper after forty-eight hours' notice. The Speaker proposes the motion for leave to introduce the bill when its sponsor wishes to proceed. This motion is deemed adopted without debate or amendment. The member sponsoring the bill may give a succinct explanation of the provisions of the bill at this point, but usually a minister presenting a government bill does not take this opportunity.

When a bill is introduced, the question "That this bill be read a first time and be printed" is deemed adopted without debate or amendment. The bill is then placed on the Order Paper for a second reading. Every bill must receive three separate readings on three different sitting days before it can be passed, except that on urgent or extraordinary occasions a bill may be read twice or three times, or advanced two or more stages, in one day.

After the first reading, the bills are printed in both English and French. Each bill must be read twice and referred to a committee before any amendment can be offered; however, in exceptional circumstances, a government bill may be referred to a committee before the second reading on motion of the government and at the discretion of the House. Ordinarily it will be referred to the appropriate standing committee, but it may be directed to a legislative committee or to a joint committee of the House and Senate. An appropriation bill, dealing with government expenditures, is referred to a committee of the whole after expenditure estimates on which the bill is based have been studied by the appropriate standing committees. At the second reading, the principle and purpose of the bill, but not its specific provisions, is debated and either accepted or rejected.

At the committee stage, the bill is considered clause by clause, and each clause can be amended. Amendments must be relevant to the subject matter and must not be outside the scope of the particular clause under consideration. They must be consistent with the provisions of the bill as agreed upon to that point by the committee. An amendment to delete a clause is improper, since the same effect can be achieved by voting against it.

At the conclusion of its consideration, the committee reports the bill to the House, with or without amendments. Forty-eight hours must then elapse, unless otherwise ordered by the House, before the reported bill can be considered. If the bill is reported from a committee of the whole, it must be concurred in without further amendment or debate at this stage. The House may amend, debate, insert or restore any clause in bills reported from other committees. After a bill has been amended or there has been debate on a proposed amendment at the report stage, it is set down on the Order Paper for third reading and passage at the next sitting of the House. If no amendment is proposed at the report stage, and in the case of appropriation bills reported from a committee of the whole, a motion "That the bill be now read a third time and passed" may be made at the same sitting. When proceedings at the report stage on any bill have been concluded a motion "That the bill, as amended, be concurred in" or "That the bill be concurred in" is put and adopted without amendment or debate.

A minister may, usually after having secured the agreement of the

House leaders of the other parties represented in the House, propose an allotment of days or hours for the proceedings at any stage of the passing of a public bill.

After a bill has received third reading and passed, it is sent to the Senate with a request that it be passed by the Upper House. Members of the Senate debate the bill and may make amendments before passing it back to the Commons. Any amendments made by the Senate are placed on the Order Paper. If the House does not concur in the Senate's amendments, it adopts a motion that states its reasons. Should the Senate still wish its amendments to be adopted, it communicates this to the House of Commons. An impasse at this stage may be referred to a conference of representatives of the two Houses. However, the Senate usually yields in the case of an impasse, or the bill fails.

The final stage before any bill becomes law is its presentation to the Crown's representative, the Governor General, or to his or her deputy, for the Royal Assent.

22. Private Bills

Private bills are distinguished from public bills in that they relate directly to the affairs of private persons or corporate entities and not to matters of general public policy or to the community at large. Private bills, which must be initiated on petition of the parties concerned and can be sponsored only by private members and not a minister of the Crown, can be introduced in either the Senate or the Commons, but current practice is that almost all such bills are introduced in the Senate. When the Speaker informs the House that a private bill has been brought from the Senate, the bill is deemed to have been read a first time and is ordered for a second reading and reference to a standing committee at the next sitting of the House. Private bills follow the procedure for private members' bills. After first reading, they are placed at the bottom of the order of precedence on the Order Paper.

In general, the Standing Orders applicable to public bills apply to private bills. After the second reading, a private bill is referred to the appropriate standing committee, which is empowered to call in the interested parties to establish or clarify the facts upon which the bill is founded. This is an important step, as private bills are usually based on considerations which take no account of public policy, and the House must be made aware of any proposed provisions of the bill that may run counter to such policy. After the committee has considered the bill it reports its findings to the House.

In addition to the procedures followed in the House, all applications to Parliament for private bills must be advertised by a notice published in the *Canada Gazette*, and a similar notice must be published in newspapers in the principal territories which would be affected by the bill, if passed. The parties applying for the bill must also pay certain fees set out in the Standing Orders.

23. Private Members' Bills

Private members' bills are public bills introduced by members who are not ministers of the Crown. The procedure for scheduling consideration of such bills is different from that outlined in the discussion of the legislative process, but the procedure for debate, amendment and passage is the same.

A private member's bill must be drafted in correct legal language, and a member can seek the assistance of the Legislative Counsel in drafting the bill. The Legislative Counsel must then certify the bill is in order. After certification, the member must give forty-eight hours' notice of his or her intention to introduce the bill. After introduction and first reading, the bill is placed on the Order Paper in the category of "Private Members' Business – Items outside the Order of Precedence."

While government bills are debated in the order the government wishes, the order in which private members' bills are debated at second reading is determined by the drawing of lots. The first draw in any session occurs within two days after thirty members have each introduced a bill or given notice of a motion. The names of the sponsoring members are drawn by the Deputy Speaker, and the first name drawn is ranked first in the order of precedence, the second ranked second, and so on.

After each draw, the bills and motions are considered by the Standing Committee on Procedure and House Affairs, which decides, after consulting with the sponsoring members, which (if any) of them, up to a maximum of five bills and five motions at any one time, are to be put to a vote in the House.

In the House, each private member's bill placed in the order of precedence is debated at the time specified in the Standing Orders. A bill selected to come to a vote by the Standing Committee on Procedure and House Affairs is debated for one hour, then, should the question not be resolved in that period, it is moved to the bottom of the order of precedence. (Bills not selected as votable are dropped from the Order Paper after one hour of debate.) Once the votable bill works its way back to the top of the order, the debate can continue for another hour, then the bill drops to the bottom again. No private member's bill can be debated for longer than three hours at second reading; it is then put to a vote. The time allowed for the committee stage is unrestricted, but the time allotted for report stage and third reading is limited under the Standing Orders. The hour set aside for private members' business during the daily sitting of the House may be suspended for various reasons set out in the Standing Orders, including the sponsoring member's absence.

24. Reports
All business transacted in each daily sitting of the House is recorded in the *Journals*, and a verbatim account of the proceedings is reported in the *Debates*, commonly called *Hansard*.

PART II

Rules and Usages for
Assemblies Generally

25. Rules

Every assembly of people who are meeting together to consider matters of common interest has to have clear and well-understood rules to govern its proceedings. These may be the formal Standing Orders of the House of Commons, discussed briefly in the last chapter, or an abbreviated and simplified system adapted for relatively small and informal bodies. All such rules, however, serve to ensure that everyone present at the assembly who has the right to be there has the opportunity to express an opinion; that the rights of a minority are respected; that clear decisions or conclusions are reached on the issues raised on the basis of a free majority vote; and as far as possible that proceedings are governed by an assessment of the issues rather than by personality factors.

Government bodies, public companies and most important organizations are governed foremost by statutes or by a constitution or charter. Such governing laws cannot be changed at the will of the body they govern, but only by the superior legislative authority that enacted them. Generally speaking, all bodies do possess, however, either the stated or implicit right to make other rules, regulations and by-laws needed to ensure their existence and usefulness. It is essential for any organization intending to have a continuous existence to establish and confirm as early as possible the rules under which it will function.

26. Changing the Rules

If at any time it becomes necessary or advisable to change the rules, care must be taken that the changes are not made haphazardly. Suggested alterations should be referred to a committee for detailed consideration. When all of the changes have been worked out by the committee, notice should be given at one meeting of the organization that at the next or a subsequent meeting a motion will be introduced that proposes these changes. All active members should then be advised in detail of the changes intended so that they can come to the meeting fully informed.

As well, members should be informed in advance of any other proposed changes to an organization that will be debated at an upcoming meeting, such as an enlargement of objectives, changes in membership qualifications or fees, and the like, and no innovative changes should be put into effect until after they have been approved by the members.

27. Suspension of Rules

Occasionally it may be necessary to suspend certain rules for the sake of smooth functioning, but this should be restricted to cases of extreme urgency, usually when time is limited or when it is necessary to deal with an extraordinary item not provided for in routine business. A motion for the suspension of a rule for a specific purpose should be moved and seconded, and it is customary to insist upon unanimous assent. When the purposes for which a suspension was made have been achieved, the suspended rule returns to full force and effect. For instance, if urgency has not permitted giving the number of days' notice of a meeting called for in the by-laws, the first business of that meeting should be the passage of a motion suspending the rule for that particular meeting and declaring the meeting duly called and regularly constituted. For subsequent meetings, the rule again applies.

28. Assemblies

The business of every legislative and deliberative assembly, every municipal council, association, religious assembly and synod, and every other body of people gathered together for agreed objectives, is transacted at a "meeting," "sitting," or "session." A "meeting" is the time between the assembling or convening of a body until the close of or adjournment of its proceedings. However, the word is used informally to describe a variety of forms of assembly. Properly, a "sitting" is the daily meeting of Parliament or of any other body whose affairs are conducted daily in a regular way over a period of time. The term "session" describes the duration of several meetings or sittings of a legislative or other deliberative body which assembles at a fixed time and, after several days or weeks or months, comes to a close by dissolution, prorogation or other formal action. Many other bodies meet once a week, a month, or even annually for the transaction of their business, in which event the word "meeting" is used to describe their assembly. If any such meeting must be adjourned until another day to complete its business, the next meeting is in effect the same meeting and should have the same agenda, as if there had been no break in the proceedings.

29. Notice of Meetings

Every person entitled to attend a meeting must be informed in advance of the day, time and place at which the meeting will be held. Whether meetings are held irregularly, or more or less regularly but not necessarily always on the same day or time or at the same place, potential participants should receive a notice with all necessary information well in advance of the meeting date. This is particularly important when those qualified to attend live at some distance from where the meeting is being held.

In the case of a session, or of a series of meetings to be held consecutively within a specified period, one notice will usually suffice, provided it contains all of the information necessary to permit those concerned to organize their time and arrange to attend the various sittings.

The notice of a meeting should include information about the nature of the business to be dealt with. If possible, copies of reports or other supporting papers relating to the matters to be considered should be attached so that potential participants can give the issues thought prior to the meeting.

30. The Presiding Officer

Every body of people assembled for the purpose of discussion, deliberation, making decisions and promoting certain objectives must be presided over by one person—the chair.* This person, whose role corresponds broadly with that of the Speaker of the House of Commons, may be given another title according to the usage, rule or law that governs a particular assembly, but the rights, duties and responsibilities of the role are in all cases similar. "President" is the term generally used for persons appointed or elected for a fixed period as the presiding officers of societies, associations, corporate bodies and the like. "Mayor," "warden" and "reeve" are titles applied to those heading municipal or other territorial councils, while clubs and religious organizations have designations peculiar to themselves.

While a meeting is in progress all remarks must be addressed to the presiding officer by the appropriate title, e.g., Mayor, Mr. President, and so on. It is always correct to address the occupant of the chair simply as Mr. or Madam Chair, for regardless of any other title, he or she is a presiding officer for the purposes of the meeting.

31. Absence of Presiding Officer

It is usual, and good, practice to elect or appoint a deputy chair or vice-chair or vice-president or other officer who can take the place of the regular presiding officer in the event of the latter's absence. The deputy possesses all the rights, duties and responsibilities of the officer he or she is temporarily replacing.

Should circumstances arise in which both the regular presiding officer and the deputy are unavoidably absent, the assembly may appoint a chair *pro tem*. This is done after the meeting approves a motion calling upon another person to act as chair. If the regular presiding officer appears in the course of a meeting which is being chaired by a temporary appointee, the latter concludes the item of business under consideration, then steps down in favour of the regular chair.

---

* While the term "chair" properly applies to the chair in which the presiding officer sits, it is now an acceptable term for the person whose role is to preside over the meeting. It avoids the assumption that this person is a man.

32. Duties of the Chair

The chair, however named, occupies an important position in any assembly. The chair calls the meeting to order to begin the proceedings; announces the items of business in the order in which they appear on the agenda; reads the motions to the meeting as they are put so that they can be formally debated; submits motions or other proposals for final decision by vote; and having determined the sense of the meeting announces that the motion or proposal has been carried or lost. The chair adjourns the meeting if a further consecutive meeting is required, or closes it if all the business of the present meeting has been accomplished.

The chair must decide, subject to appeal, all questions of order and procedure, and must at all times preserve the order and decorum essential to calm deliberation, effective use of the available time, and general agreement that fair and equitable processes have led to acceptable conclusions.

In large, formal meetings the chair ensures the efficient conduct of the business before the assembly but does not participate in debate. The chair must remain objective and impartial, acting strictly as an umpire of proceedings. Removing the chair from active participation is necessary in view of the chair's role in regulating the conduct of the gathering and in ensuring that conflicting opinion receives equal expression. In these circumstances the chair has no vote, but may exercise a deciding or casting vote if the vote is tied.

In less formal gatherings and in committees the chair, while carrying out all of the usual functions in conducting the proceedings, enjoys the same right as any other member to participate in discussion and to vote on any issue. However, should the chair wish to propose a motion, he or she should step down in favour of the vice-chair (or to any other temporary chair if the latter is not present) and should not resume chairing until the motion has been resolved.

All persons assuming a chair's duties should:

(a) have reasonable assurance that they have the time and inclination for the role;

(b) have a sufficient working knowledge of the rules of

43

procedure to permit them to carry out their duties with confidence and to the satisfaction of their associates;

(c) be familiar with the constitution, by-laws, rules and usages of the organization they serve; and

(d) be able to be tactful and decisive in ensuring effective and orderly progress.

Principal officers can have other duties to perform in addition to acting as the chair of meetings. They should interest themselves in preparations for meetings and be assured that all needed papers such as reports are available or have been distributed. Similarly, they should see that all decisions for action agreed to at meetings of the group are implemented. The chair is customarily the signing officer for official papers produced on the organization's behalf and will sometimes be called upon to act as the organization's representative and spokesperson in contacts with other bodies and with the press.

33. Choosing the Presiding Officer

In most cases an organization's principal officer is elected or appointed in accordance with laws or specific procedures detailed in the organization's constitution or by-laws, or sometimes even simply according to long-accepted custom. An officer so chosen automatically presides at assemblies of the members unless specific alternative arrangements are made.

If an assembly is brought together without a chair already designated, one of its earliest actions should be to choose someone to preside. Anyone who has taken some part in bringing the group together should call for the nomination of a chair, a chair *pro tem.*, or of some other officer or officers, permanent or temporary, according to the circumstances. After a nomination has been made and seconded, it is voted upon. Usually the nominee readily agrees to accept, but can decline, the nomination, in which case another nominee must be proposed. If two or more nominees are proposed, a vote is taken on each in the order in which they were proposed, i.e., the first name is voted upon, and if rejected, the second name is put to the vote, and so forth. If the votes for the first nominees are equal, the motion is deemed to be lost and the next name is proposed for a decision.

If a meeting is convened for a specific purpose, the duties of the person chosen to preside are deemed to have been carried out at the conclusion of that meeting or whenever the business of the meeting has been accomplished. A chair chosen *pro tem.* at the inaugural meeting of a body intending to have a continuing existence acts as such until regular procedures have been set up and a permanent presiding officer has been elected.

By-laws or regulations usually set the term of a presiding officer and may provide that the office cannot be held by the same person for more than a specified number of successive terms.

34. Quorum

A quorum is the minimum number of people who must be present to validate the transaction of business. In legislative bodies a quorum is established by statute or standing order and is usually many less than the total number of members of such bodies. Other organizations may specify the number of a quorum in a by-law or regulation. If no provision is made, a quorum is a majority of the total number of members. It is good practice to have the number of a quorum clearly fixed, particularly for large groups; the attendance of four of a committee of six can usually be expected, but more than half of a group of a hundred may very well not attend.

Official business cannot be transacted in the absence of a quorum. Should members leave in the course of a meeting that has begun with a quorum, proceedings must cease at the point at which the number attending falls below a quorum. The chair at this point adjourns the meeting to a later date if items remain on the agenda that still require decision. (There is an informal procedure in this circumstance allowing for interim decisions, but they cannot be regarded as the official decisions of the body nor be acted upon until they have been ratified at a subsequent meeting with a quorum present.)

The importance of a quorum arises from the need to avoid any appearance of action by a minority which might commit the whole group without its assent or the opportunity to advance dissenting opinion.

35. Order of Business

An order of business, or agenda, should be prepared in advance of every meeting. Ordinarily it is the duty of the secretary, or of the officer who carries out secretarial duties, to compile a list of the items to be dealt with, to ensure that it is in the hands of the chair before the meeting begins, and it is desirable also that copies be made available for all in attendance. The order of the items of business will usually follow an accustomed pattern, beginning with the reading of the minutes of the preceding meeting, then reports, followed by pending business and new business in a convenient arrangement.

The business should be called item by item by the chair, following the order in which they appear on the agenda. The chair should not depart from the pre-arranged order without a good reason for doing so, such as the delayed attendance of a member who may be important to the discussion. A change in the order of business should in any event be made only after establishing that the meeting as a whole does not object.

An agenda properly prepared in advance and circulated to all in attendance at the start facilitates the conduct of the meeting, as fore-knowledge encourages forethought. As well, it discourages the introduction of irrelevancies and avoids the unnecessary anticipation of questions scheduled for later consideration.

While there is no rule governing the introduction at a meeting of new questions not contained in the prepared agenda, the chair should be prepared to deal with the situation if it arises. At a formal meeting the chair has the right to decline to admit such questions for consideration, as members have had no notice that they would be raised and they may be inadequately informed to deal with them properly. On the other hand, at smaller or committee meetings the chair might permit consideration of a new issue if time permits and there is no objection to adding it to the agenda.

36. Motions

A motion is a proposal placed before a meeting, and properly all decisions made at the meeting and recorded in the minutes should be on the basis of motions either adopted or defeated. A motion that has been adopted becomes the decision of the meeting. There should be only one main or substantive motion before a meeting at any one time.

Whenever possible, a motion should be worded in affirmative terms and it should express fully and unambiguously the intent of the mover. It should not be preceded by a preamble ("Whereas . . ." or "In order to . . ."), since these represent opinions which are arguable or make statements which may or may not be factual. A motion is made by a member who, after being recognized by the chair, rises and, addressing the chair, simply states "I move that. . . ." An important motion, or one containing a number of considerations, should be prepared in writing and given to the chair, preferably in advance of the meeting. All main motions should be seconded by another member making a statement to that effect. Unless it is seconded, a motion is not open to consideration.

After a motion has been seconded, the chair restates it. This puts the question to the meeting and opens the debate. After the motion has been put, a motion may be withdrawn by its mover and seconder *only* with the assent of the meeting as a whole. In the course of debate the motion may be amended in various ways, or action may be taken to delay or defer its effect, but it must remain before the meeting until it is finally disposed of in one way or another.

When a vote has been taken and the motion declared either carried or lost, that decision becomes formally the decision of the body in question and its adoption is recorded in the minutes of the meeting. Once decided a question cannot be brought up again at the same meeting, but if it should become necessary to rescind a motion that has been passed, notice of intention to do so can be given at one meeting or in advance in some other way. A motion for rescinding is then introduced and dealt with at a subsequent meeting. Ordinarily a motion that has once failed cannot be reintroduced; however, the decision can be later reconsidered (see below) or another motion of similar intent but differing in some particulars can be considered at the discretion of the chair.

The democratic right to introduce a proposition in the form of a motion, and to have a full debate and a free vote on the matter, carries with it an obligation on the part of the majority to respect its own decisions, just as the minority is obliged to accept and respect the decisions of the majority. In other words, a decision reached by due process must be recognized and observed as such by all concerned; if it calls for action, that action must be taken.

37. Reconsideration

Procedures are sometimes provided not only for rescinding a motion that has been adopted, but also for reconsidering a motion that failed. A reconsideration rule usually requires advance notice in writing that a question will be reconsidered at the next meeting. The provision is a useful one, in that conclusions occasionally may be reached too hastily or on the basis of inadequate information, and a later review may well be in the general interest. However, reconsideration should not be allowed except upon due notice and formal motion, and it is customary to insist on a two-thirds majority vote on a motion to reconsider.

38. Amendments

Anyone qualified to debate a motion who finds that, while it is acceptable in principle, it is deficient in any one or more of its terms, can propose a motion to amend it. An amendment can change a word or words in a motion, may add words to it or delete words from it. It must not merely negate a motion, since this result is best achieved by voting against it. An amending motion may be introduced by stating "I move to amend the motion by substituting the words . . . with the words . . . so that the motion will read . . ." The amending motion must be seconded.

An amending motion must be strictly relevant to the main motion and be made while the main motion is under consideration. It must not alter in a significant way the principle embodied in the main motion, but merely vary the terms of one or more particulars. The chair must decide any question about the propriety of a proposed amendment. Not infrequently, a motion to amend will be introduced which is in reality a new motion, and the chair should act promptly and firmly to rule it out of order.

Just as an amendment may be moved to a main motion, so can an amendment be moved to an amendment. The conditions that apply to an original amendment also apply to such a secondary amendment or subamendment: It may propose a variation in the terms of the original amendment but it must not materially alter the underlying intent of either the original amendment or the main motion. Usually only two amendments to a question – an amendment and a subamendment – are allowed at the same time. When one or both have been dealt with, a further amendment or subamendment, as the case may be, can be entertained by the chair.

When there has been a main motion, an amendment and a subamendment, the procedure is as follows:

When the chair is satisfied that the subamendment has been fully discussed, he or she puts the question "Shall the subamendment carry?" If it does, discussion continues on the amendment, as amended, at the conclusion of which the chair puts the question "Shall the amendment as amended carry?"; or, if the subamendment failed, the question is "Shall the amendment carry?" In either case, if the motion carries, discussion then moves to the main question as amended. The chair's final question is "Shall the main motion as amended carry?"; or, if the amendment was defeated "Shall the main motion carry?"

Note that this procedure is always in reverse order, from subamendment through amendment to the main motion. An amendment can be introduced at any stage before the question is put on the main motion, provided there is not more than one amendment and one subamendment before the meeting at one time. Any member wishing to move an amendment that is not in order at the time because there are already two amendments before the meeting can still state the intention of the motion, as the proposal might affect the vote on those motions awaiting decision.

Providing for the introduction of amendments is an important procedural measure, but in the interests of clarity and expediency, it is wise to avoid undue complication. This can sometimes be accomplished by forethought and consultation in the preparation of the main motion.

It is, again, the responsibility of the chair to guide the meeting through the amending process to a clearly understood result that has the support of the majority.

39. Notice of Motion

If a substantial issue is to be raised affecting the constitution, policies or procedures of a body, it is always advisable, and in some cases

49

mandatory, that notice be given at one meeting that this issue will be introduced by motion at the next or a subsequent meeting. The notice is merely a statement of intention and can be made by any member at an appropriate time in the proceedings. It requires no seconder and is not at that time debatable.

The purpose of giving notice is to permit the members of an organization to consider and prepare for the question or questions that will be placed before them for consideration. This facilitates discussion and contributes to efficient and satisfactory resolution of the matter. When an intention to introduce a motion has been announced, the item should be placed on the agenda of the meeting at which it is to be dealt with. The notice of this meeting should refer to the item and, if possible, should include the actual text of the motion to be introduced, and, if needed, explanatory material should be appended.

In some organizations, constitutions or by-laws dictate that, for certain classes of motions, notice must be given of an intention to introduce a motion at a specific time or number of days before it can be considered.

Notice is not generally necessary in the case of amendments to a motion, although substantive questions may arise in connection with a motion for which notice has been given. If these new questions are known in advance of the meetings, prior notice of them can be given if doing so will facilitate the meeting.

40. Motions for Special Purposes

In addition to a main motion, which offers a proposal, and amendments to vary the terms of a main motion, which are all debatable, there are certain motions that can be made during a debate and which for the most part are not debatable or amendable. The principal class of such motions are called "dilatory" motions, since their effect is to supersede, delay or postpone the consideration of a question. They may be put in the course of debate, but not so as to interrupt a speaker who has the floor.

The principal subsidiary motions are as follows:

(a) *Motion to Adjourn* – A motion to adjourn the debate or the meeting is always in order, must be seconded, but is not debatable. It is a tool

50

to have a decision on a question deferred. If a motion to adjourn carries, the matter under consideration must be put aside, but it can be reinstated at a later meeting. The current meeting ceases and is reconvened to resume discussion of the remaining agenda items at another time. If the motion fails, the meeting proceeds as though no interruption had occurred.

(b) *Proceeding to Next Business* – A motion to proceed to the next business, or calling for the reading of the orders of the day, if carried, also sets aside the question being considered and the meeting proceeds to the next item on the agenda. If it fails, discussion resumes. The motion must be seconded and must be put to the meeting immediately.

(c) *The Previous Question* – The motion known as "the previous question" is made in the form "I move that the question be now put," or more colloquially, "I call for the question." Its object is to prevent the proposing of amendments or any other intervening action and so force a direct vote on the main motion. The motion must be seconded and can be debated, but it cannot be amended. If it carries, the question on the main motion must be put immediately and a decision reached. A defeat of the motion means, in effect, that the main motion may not be now put to the question, and it is superseded. It may, however, be revived on a future day, as the defeat of the motion merely binds the chair not to put the main question at that time.

The motion "that the question be now put" should be used with caution and with a clear understanding of the end it is intended to accomplish, which is that debate comes to an end and there is no further action prior to a vote on the issue in question, or if the motion fails that the issue will be temporarily set aside.

(d) *Deferment* – Motions to postpone to a specified time, or indefinitely, or to table, are admissible, but are uncommon in Canadian practice. Questions that have been properly put before a meeting should be resolved one way or another, but if circumstances arise that make it desirable to defer consideration of an issue for the time being or indefinitely, a motion to this effect can be made; it must be seconded and it is debatable. If the motion carries, the motion to which it applies is

51

removed from debate along with any amendments that have been moved. It cannot be reintroduced until either the time specified in the motion to defer or until it is later revived on motion.

A motion to table a question is similar in its effect, and is usually used to put aside a question so that more urgent business can be attended to. If a motion to table is carried, the main motion to which it is applied is laid aside, together with any amendments to it, but its consideration may be resumed at any time on motion that the matter be taken from the table. The latter motion must be decided immediately without amendment or debate.

(e) *Reference, or Committal* – If it should be decided that a subject demands fuller consideration than can be given in a regular meeting, a motion can be made that it be referred, or committed, to a standing or special committee. Such a motion may be amended and debated, but only the issue of reference or committal, not the main question. It cannot be superseded by a motion to postpone or for "the previous question."

It should be noted that some of these special motions, particularly those to postpone and to table, are not drawn from Canadian parliamentary practice, and they should be accepted only if there has been general prior agreement to their use and effect. These and other rules of procedure have been developed in the United States, together with a whole system of usage and precedence.

For the purposes of the great majority of meetings, where those attending cannot be expected to have familiarity with all the possibilities of complex procedures, it is usually sufficient and advantageous to adopt the simplest rules that meet the circumstance, based on or adapted from those of the Canadian Parliament.

41. Debate

Meetings are held to permit those who qualify to express their views on the matters raised for consideration; all members have such a right provided they are prepared to exercise it within the agreed framework of rules and usages. In Parliament and many legislative or other public bodies, there are rules that limit the number of times a member or participant may speak and the length of speeches, so that the time available can be shared fairly. In less formal or smaller bodies and in committees these restrictions are not generally imposed, although the chair should use discretion to prevent one person from dominating the meeting or unfairly using up the time and the patience of the members.

A member, having risen to signal a desire to speak, must await recognition by the chair. If two or more signal at the same time, the chair will call upon the one who first caught his or her attention and should indicate at that time the order in which the others who wish to speak may have the floor.

All remarks should be addressed to the chair. Even if a member who has the floor wishes to ask a question of some other member, the question should properly be directed to the chair, as the chair has the right to determine whether the question, or any other matter, is in order. The chair can decline a question to be put or any other action taken if in his or her opinion it would be contrary to the rules or would offend propriety. The chair's ruling can be appealed.

Remarks and arguments must be relevant to the question being considered. The chair is the judge of relevancy and can interrupt a speaker who is deviating unduly from the main thread of the discussion. Otherwise a speaker has the right to be heard without interruption, unless committing a breach of order or contravening the rules of the assembly or meeting. In this case, any member may interject and the speaker must cease until the matter has been dealt with.

Needless to say, remarks made in the course of discussion should be in good taste, be incapable of being misinterpreted, and should give offence to no one.

The purposes of any meeting will be served when all members act with propriety in the course of debate. More latitude can be allowed in small and informal meetings, but in all cases the rights and sensibilities of all participants must be observed and respected.

42. Putting the Question
When a motion or an issue has been debated, and the chair senses that the meeting is prepared to make its decision, he or she inquires whether

the meeting is ready for the question. Alternatively, the chair can halt proceedings at a specified time if there is a prior agreement to place such a limit on the debate.

If there is no objection to the question being put, the chair says "The question is as follows . . ." and then reads the motion or describes the issue. The chair then calls for those in favour to so signal, then those opposed. Even if it is obvious that the majority is in favour, the chair must still call on those opposed to so signal, as there are frequently those who wish to make their objection clear.

43. Methods of Voting

There are several ways a vote can be registered:

(a) *Voice* — The chair can ask those in favour to say "aye" or "yea," then those opposed to say "nay," announcing that the ayes or the nays have it, as the case may be, and declaring the motion either carried or lost. This method has the disadvantage that, when there is anything like an equal division of opinion, the chair can find it difficult to determine which side is the majority. The chair may be challenged and a motion introduced for a second vote in a different method. It is always unsatisfactory to conduct a second vote, as some participants may be influenced by the first vote to change their minds for personal or expedient reasons. A noticeable difference in the outcome of the two votes can leave some participants with the suspicion of carelessness or even manipulation.

(b) *Show of Hands* — By far the most common method of voting in ordinary meetings is by a show of hands. Those for and against the motion are in turn asked to raise their right hands; the hands are counted, the result announced, and the motion declared either carried or lost.

(c) *Standing Vote* — For certain issues it can be appropriate or important to identify those in favour or opposed, in which case a motion should be introduced for a standing vote. If the motion carries, those supporting and those opposing the proposal being considered are asked, in turn, to stand, and they are counted. As this method emphasizes the division of opinion, it should be used with caution.

(d) *Ballot* – The organization's by-laws or regulations may require that votes on certain specified matters are registered by ballot, or a meeting can decide on motion that ballots are cast on a particular issue. In this case, after the question has been put, all those who are qualified to vote are given a ballot paper on which to record their vote. The completed ballots are then collected and counted (enumerated), and the chair announces that the motion has either carried or lost. The numerical count does not have to be announced unless specifically required or the meeting requests it be announced.

(e) *Mail Ballot* – Large organizations, where full attendance at a meeting is virtually impossible, can specify in their by-laws or regulations that a mail ballot must be held on certain major issues so that everyone who is qualified has an opportunity to register an opinion. Firm rules should be drawn up to govern this procedure, and scrutineers must be appointed to supervise the vote.

Regardless of the procedure used, any vote must be, and must be seen to be, carried out with absolute fairness and to have an unequivocal result.

For certain important issues, the by-laws or regulations often state that there must be a two-thirds majority for a motion to carry; in routine business a simple majority is sufficient. Unless the rules state otherwise, the chair has the same voting rights as any other member. As well, when the vote is equal or tied, the chair is usually given a second or casting vote. If the chair does not have this right, then the motion is lost when the votes are tied.

When routine items are being decided upon, or when it is obvious to the chair that there is no objection to a proposal being discussed, the chair can dispense with the formal vote and simply say "If there is no objection . . ." and assume general assent. Should someone object to this assumption, a vote must be taken.

44. Order

In formal assemblies the word "order" has more than one meaning. The chair calls the meeting to order to quiet the participants and get their attention focused on the business of the meeting. The by-laws or regulations of organizations set out an order of procedure. Order also means decorum and plain good behaviour. It is the chair's duty to see that order in all these senses is observed and preserved.

If in the course of debate a member says or does something that is contrary to the rules or established custom, the chair should immediately call him or her to order. The simple admonition "Order, please" is usually sufficient to correct a minor breach, but for more serious infractions, the chair may need to address the person by name and say, "You are out of order." The person named must then stop speaking and sit down while the chair explains the point of order. The chair's ruling is not debatable, and it is usually accepted. It may still be challenged, however, on a properly seconded motion to dissent from the ruling. This motion is not debatable and must be put to the vote immediately. If it receives majority support, the chair's ruling is overturned.

Any member can at any time rise on a point of order, interrupting a speaker if necessary, to point out a breach of the rules. The speaker should sit down while the point is cleared. The chair must then rule whether a breach of order has occurred.

It is the duty of the chair to be ready and able at all times to maintain order, that is, to ensure the meeting proceeds and that deliberations remain calm. If there is a disturbance, the chair must courteously halt the meeting, interrupting a speaker if necessary, call for order and, if needed, admonish the offenders. If order cannot be restored this simply, the chair can recess the meeting for a brief period or, in the event of a serious disturbance, adjourn the meeting to another day.

Serious disturbances are rare, but are not unknown, and anyone chairing a meeting must be prepared to be calm, firm and discreet in exercising the chair's authority.

It should be noted that the chair does not have the authority to discipline an offending member or to impose penalties. If this course of action seems to be necessary, a motion setting out the discipline or penalty must be moved, seconded and receive assent from a substantial majority. If the breach of order requiring discipline occurs at a meeting designed only for qualified members, and non-members are present, the chair can request that all non-members leave and can enforce that request by whatever measures are necessary.

Slander is the spoken and libel is the written defamation of the character of another. Both are actionable in law, and everyone participating in a meeting must be alert to the possible serious consequences of intemperate or harmful statements.

45. Privilege

Questions of privilege can be raised at any point during a debate, as long as no speaker is interrupted. These questions usually have to do with a violation or a perceived violation of the rights or interests of the meeting or organization as a whole or of a member personally. The chair must decide if the matter is, in fact, a question of privilege and therefore subject to appeal. If the chair rules that it is, the matter must be dealt with immediately before debate on the main issue is resumed.

The word "privileged" also applies to remarks made in a closed meeting that, if made publicly, could be considered actionable. Statements made in Parliament, for example, are considered privileged even though the same statements made outside Parliament might be considered defamatory. It is unwise for ordinary assemblies or meetings to assume any right of privilege, as legal action could still be taken, and it would be up to the courts to decide the matter.

46. Closing the Meeting

When all the business and purposes of a meeting have been attended to and the chair is satisfied there is no other business that should be dealt with, he or she simply announces that the meeting is closed or terminated. The chair does not need a motion to this effect to be proposed nor any other authority.

There are, however, other circumstances that can require a meeting to be ended or halted:

(a) If the by-laws or other regulations state that meetings must conclude by a specified time, the chair must stop the meeting at that time regardless of whether its business has been accomplished. Any items remaining on the agenda are carried forward to the next or a subsequent meeting, *unless* a motion is adopted abrogating or abolishing the rule for that particular meeting. If, during a meeting, a motion is passed that the meeting conclude at a specified time, the chair must follow the instruction.

(b) A motion to adjourn is always in order, and if it is passed, the meeting immediately comes to a halt, regardless of the stage of the proceedings.

(c) If the chair deems it necessary to interrupt a meeting, for example to obtain information needed by the meeting, he or she can recess the meeting or *suggest* that it adjourn to another day. To have effect, this suggestion must be adopted by other members of the meeting after a motion has properly been moved, seconded and voted upon.

(d) The chair may, on his or her own initiative, recess or adjourn a disorderly meeting he or she cannot call to order.

(e) Should the meeting fail to reach quorum at its outset, or lose quorum part-way through its proceedings, the chair should adjourn it to another day. The meeting can proceed as an information meeting only; any decisions made are not binding and cannot be put into effect until ratified by a properly constituted meeting.

47. Minutes and Records

Minutes are a record of proceedings and they are an integral part of the operation of any organization. The responsibility for preparing and maintaining the minutes belongs to the secretary, recording secretary, clerk or other officer specifically appointed for the purpose. The minute-taker writes notes during the meeting and prepares a typed or clean copy of the complete minutes as soon as possible after the meeting. Copies of all minutes should be kept in consecutive order in a binder, where they serve as an important record of the organization's proceedings and decisions.

The minutes of each meeting should record the place, date and time at which it was held; the name of the presiding officer; either a list of those attending or some other evidence of a quorum, and any other relevant detail, such as the attendance of guests or regrets sent by members unable to attend.

The minutes should accurately record the actions taken and decisions made by the meeting in regard to the items of business it considered. They should not attempt to be a verbatim account of the meeting, but can include references to the major points made in the course of debate. Usually, speakers are not identified, but their names can be recorded if that information is directly relevant to the issue being debated. The minute-taker should aim for completeness, clarity and succinctness.

The first item of business at most meetings is the reading and approval, or confirmation, of the minutes of the previous meeting. If an error is detected, the necessary correction should be made at once and the minutes approved as corrected after a motion to that effect has been moved and seconded. There should be no debate on the policy or merits of a question dealt with in the minutes, and remarks on the minutes must relate strictly to the matter of the error.

If possible, the minutes of the previous meeting should be distributed in advance to those entitled to receive them. This reminds members who attended the last meeting of the business transacted, and informs members who were not present. It also reduces the time required for dealing with the minutes, since they can be taken as read and approved or confirmed by a simple motion.

After the minutes have been approved, the copy to be used as the permanent record should be signed by the presiding officer.

Other papers regarding an organization's business, such as reports, financial statements, and so on, must also be preserved by the secretary or recording officer or another official appointed to the task. These records should be available for inspection for legitimate purposes by any member of the organization in good standing. Usually, such a request is channelled through a senior officer who can ascertain whether it is a legitimate request.

Reports or other documents vital to the business of a meeting should be referred to in the minutes of that meeting and appended to them as an integral part of the minutes.

48. Committees

Committees are important bodies as they can give an issue more detailed and effective consideration than is possible by the whole assembly. They can spend whatever time is necessary to investigate an issue or to consult with others before coming up with one or more recommendations for the full assembly to consider.

A committee of the whole is a device used regularly by legislative bodies to allow freer debate and detailed examination of bills and reports. A motion that the body resolve itself into a committee of the whole must be passed, and then the presiding officer steps down in favour of a chair appointed to serve the committee of the whole. After the committee has finished its deliberations, it reports its findings and formal action is taken by the assembly. Private organizations have little need ever to meet as a committee of the whole.

Standing committees are appointed or elected to consider matters of an on-going nature, and they usually have a continuing responsibility in those areas. They can be, for example, standing committees on finance, on membership, on program, and the like. The membership of standing committees is usually revised annually or from time to time as needed.

Special committees can be appointed at any time an issue needs to be referred to a smaller body for consideration, and they exist only for the length of time they require to study the issue and make recommendations. Special committees are usually appointed after a motion to that effect is passed by the whole meeting. The chair has the right to name individuals to the special committee, including the chair of the committee, but usually does so after hearing the meeting's suggestions.

When a special committee's duties have been carried out, it can consider itself to be dissolved. If it reaches an impasse and cannot carry out its duties, a special committee can ask the main body to dissolve it.

A committee can arrange its own procedures, as long as they do not contravene the directives given by the main body or the regulations governing the main body. It can deal only with the matters referred to it and cannot go beyond its terms of reference. Its report must be made to the body that appointed it and to no other interested party unless it is specifically authorized to do so by the appointing body.

A committee can consist of any number of individuals, even one.

Committees are usually more effective if their number is small and their members chosen on the basis of their qualification to deal with the issue before the committee.

A subcommittee is part of a committee appointed to deal with an aspect of the committee's business. It is responsible to, and reports to, the committee.

An executive committee usually comprises the officers of the organization, as laid out in its by-laws or regulations. It can have wide policy-making and administrative powers, but is still answerable to the main body.

Unless otherwise stated, the quorum of a committee is a majority of its members.

49. Reports

Any report of a committee to its main body should contain all of the information the main body needs in order to come to a decision on the issue.

Standing committees' reports are often routine and informational. Any recommendations of the committee should reported to the main body, preferably in the form of motions to be debated and possibly also amended.

A special committee's report should deal exclusively with the issue or issues referred to it, stating what those issues are and what specific recommendation the committee is making. The recommendation can be made in the form of a motion, which can be debated and amended by the main body.

If the committee needs to work for a long period of time, a progress report should be made, either verbally or in writing, to the main body. In this case, no action is required, but the main body can give its committee advice or directives. A committee's final report should be in writing and distributed to members of the main body in advance of the meeting at which it will be considered.

Reports should be clear and concise. They should not detail the considerations leading to a conclusion or recommendation unless they are required to understand the issue and the committee's proposal. The report should be signed by the chair of the committee or, if the committee wants to give its report particular emphasis, by all members of the committee. Usually the chair of the committee presents it to the main body.

A report can simply be received, which means it has been accepted but that no further action on it will be taken. This is appropriate when the report is essentially informative or when the main body does not wish to take action for the time being on any proposal in the report. Receipt of the report is recorded in the minutes, and its proposals can be considered at a later date.

Reports, other than those of a committee of the whole, can be debated and amended. The main body may alter or adjust any part of any proposal in the report or can decline to accept the proposal altogether. If the meeting thinks that the report is insufficient and cannot be corrected by amendment, the report can be referred back to the committee for further study and revision.

A committee's report should be supported by a majority of committee members. If there are irreconcilable differences within the committee, the minority may issue its own report in order to set out its opposing views. The main body does not act on a minority report, however, unless it is submitted with a motion that it be adopted in place of the majority report.

50. General

How formally a meeting should be conducted depends upon what procedures are detailed in the organization's constitution or by-laws and regulations. If no procedures are detailed, the degree of formality depends upon custom and precedent. Even if there is no formal directive, it is vital that the basic rules of order are understood by all members; otherwise members can be unsure of their rights and limitations, and the validity of decisions may be open to question. Sloppy and confused procedures can lead to ill will and to ineffective conclusions.

At the same time, a fussy dependence on the minutiae of procedure can be equally frustrating and non-productive. Insistence upon a rigmarole of rules that are only marginally applicable and that many participants are not familiar with can be time-consuming and can hamper the easy flow of meaningful discussion.

The objective should be a well-understood procedure that meets but does not exceed the needs of the organization and its members in a particular circumstance.

Small groups often function best in an informal atmosphere, and even in a formal meeting it can sometimes be desirable to open a subject for informal discussion. The chair, however, should never lose control of the proceedings, no matter how informal they are, and at their conclusion the chair should be certain that any decisions reached are properly based and duly recorded.

PART III

Assemblies and Organizations

51. Lawful and Unlawful Assemblies

Section 2 of the Canadian Charter of Rights and Freedoms declares that "Everyone has the following fundamental freedoms: (a) freedom of conscience and religion; (b) freedom of thought, belief, opinion and expression, including freedom of the press and other media communication; (c) freedom of peaceful assembly; and (d) freedom of association."

Part (c) of this statement of principle gives all Canadians the right to meet together in public, but this does not mean that a group of people meeting in public cannot be charged with the criminal offence of creating a nuisance or committing a trespass. What it does mean is that as long as people have assembled for a lawful purpose, and provided they do not break any law, their meeting should not be interfered with by others who object to the purpose of the meeting.

However, the way a meeting is conducted may call into question its legality. By Canadian criminal law, an unlawful assembly is a meeting of three or more people whose conduct causes others in the neighbourhood of the meeting to fear, on reasonable grounds, either that they will disturb the peace, or that they will provoke others to disturb the peace.

As well, a lawful assembly may become an unlawful one if during the meeting there is a change in conditions which makes the meeting illegal. For example, if the meeting moves from its lawful place of assembly and trespasses on private property, it becomes an unlawful assembly.

52. Procedure at Public Meetings

When people meet together in response to a public notice or an advertisement to discuss a matter of public interest, one of the people who is responsible for convening the meeting, or who is in some way directly concerned with it, should call the meeting to order and request the nomination of a chair. A motion "That (name) take the chair" should be seconded and put to the meeting. If more than one person is nominated, each name is dealt with in the order of nomination. Whoever called the meeting to order continues to act as temporary director of the proceedings until a chair is elected.

Once the chair has been chosen, he or she calls the meeting to order and then asks the meeting to appoint a secretary to keep a record of the proceedings. When a secretary has been chosen in the same manner as the chair, he or she keeps the minutes of the meeting, carefully noting any decisions reached.

Ordinarily, a meeting proceeds with the business for which it was called only after it has been regularly constituted by the election of a chair and secretary.

To begin, the chair should read the notice or advertisement calling the meeting (if there is no such notice, the chair should inform the meeting briefly of its purpose), and then call upon those people who are especially interested in the matter to address the assembly. The chair can at his or her discretion limit the length of speeches and the number of times each person can participate in the discussion, but should make it clear to the meeting that purpose of the limit is merely to save time and to allow the widest possible expression of opinion.

If a meeting is held for a specific purpose, for example, to express an opinion on a question of the day or to promote some charitable, benevolent or other public project, the people responsible for convening the meeting should be ready with motions or propositions that will assist the assembly to come to a conclusion on the matter under discussion. However, they and the chair should avoid creating the impression that they are trying to influence the proceedings unduly.

The rules for the conduct of a public meeting are the same as those for any meeting. Motions and amendments must be properly put and debated, and decisions must be reached by due process. The chair should remain impartial and take no active part in the debate. As at every type of meeting, the chair should be firm, courteous and tactful, and be willing, within the limits of the time available, not just to allow but also to encourage the expression of all opinions. However, if the meeting becomes unruly, or the speakers act or speak improperly, the chair should interrupt and appeal for good conduct. If the meeting gets beyond the chair's control, he or she can declare it at an end. This act destroys the meeting's constitutionality, and it has no right to carry on.

When the chair believes that a subject has been fully discussed, and it appears that the meeting is ready to vote, he or she asks: "Is the meeting ready for the question?" If it is ready, the chair then asks those in favour of the motion or the proposal to raise their hands, and next asks those opposed to do the same. The votes are counted by the secretary, or sometimes by tellers who have been appointed for the purpose in advance, and the chair declares the motion carried or lost as the case may be. The secretary and the tellers, if any, still have the right to vote. In the case of a tie vote the motion is lost, but the chair may cast a deciding vote after considering its possible effect. It is preferable for the chair to vote in a way that will allow the debate to be continued at a future meeting. The chair can explain the reasons behind his or her vote.

Anyone who makes a mistake in voting should say so immediately and have the error rectified before the chair announces the final decision on the question; otherwise the vote cannot be changed. It is important that the voting procedure leads to a clear-cut result and avoids any demand that the vote be taken again.

In a large public assembly, voting usually takes place by a show of hands. A voice vote (when the chair calls for "yeas" and "nays") is usually not practical, nor is one requiring those present to rise in their places to be counted. Similarly, a ballot should be used only in exceptional circumstances when the secrecy of the individual votes is considered essential.

When the business of the meeting has been concluded, the chair asks if there are any other items of business. The chair then decides whether any such other items are admissible, on the grounds of their relevancy. If the meeting has been called for a specific purpose, the chair should not hesitate in refusing to admit clearly extraneous matters for discussion. If there is no further business, the chair formally declares the meeting closed.

53. Formation of Associations, Societies, etc.

When a number of people want to establish an association for any legitimate purpose, for example, to undertake common business interests or scholarly studies, or to pursue charitable, recreational or other objectives, the promoters of the project should first assure themselves that their idea is workable. Once they have done so, and have agreed upon a general outline, they must give notice, by advertisement or otherwise, announcing the time and place of a meeting to establish an organization.

When all those who are interested in the project have assembled, one of the promoters calls the meeting to order and calls for the election of temporary officers (a chair and secretary) for the purposes of the meeting. They are elected by the same procedure used for ordinary public assemblies (see the preceding chapter).

The chair reads the notice calling the meeting, adding whatever brief remarks he or she considers necessary, and then opens the meeting for comment from anyone attending. The meeting should be conducted informally so as to encourage free and full debate, and no rules need be imposed as long as the speakers exercise good sense and keep their comments relevant to the issue. The chair should, as usual, exercise tact and good judgement. After some preliminary discussion of a general nature, someone should propose, and another second, a formal motion as a basis of debate. Such a motion might be: "That in the opinion of this meeting it is desirable to form a society to encourage studies in Canadian literature (or whatever the objective might be)."

After a full discussion the motion should be put by the chair. If it carries, action should be taken to give substance to the decision. Someone might move: "That a committee of (such and such a number) be appointed, comprising (such and such names), to frame a constitution for a society to encourage studies in Canadian literature and to report back at a meeting to be called at (place, date and hour)." The committee can be given the task of recommending the name, nature and function of the society, or the chair can allow further brief discussion as a guide to the committee. If a name for the society has been suggested, or is considered of special importance, it can be put forward in the form of a motion and dealt with at the preliminary meeting.

The preliminary meeting then adjourns until the specified day and hour, when it resumes with the same acting chair and secretary. If they are absent, two others are appointed in their places. The acting chair calls for the minutes of the last meeting to be read and approved, then asks whether the committee appointed to frame a constitution is ready to report. If it is, the report is read aloud, usually by the committee chair. It should be a written majority report, signed by the committee chair, who should begin by stating its mandate, as follows: "The committee appointed to frame a constitution for a society to encourage studies in Canadian literature (or whatever the purpose may be) respectfully submits the following as a recommendation," and then reads the draft of the constitution. If the draft is a lengthy document, copies of it should be distributed in advance to those attending the meeting to encourage informed debate on the subject. The committee chair then moves "That the report be now considered." After this motion is seconded, put to the meeting and agreed to, the document can be debated, amended and adopted or rejected under the auspices of the acting chair of the meeting.

The report should be considered in detail, paragraph by paragraph, each of which can be discussed, approved, amended or rejected.

After the constitution has been adopted, the acting chair should call upon those present who want to become members to sign a roll or membership prepared by the secretary. Those who sign are the charter members. The acting chair can call a recess for this purpose.

After the recess, the acting chair takes the sense of the meeting — strictly speaking, of the members of the new society as they appear on the signed roll — whether to proceed right away with the election of officers. If the members agree, the acting chair asks for nominations for each of the offices set out in the constitution, usually a president, one or more vice-presidents, a secretary, a treasurer, and sometimes a council. Each nomination is voted on. If there is more than one nomination for a single office, each name is voted on in the order of nomination. On this occasion a show of hands is all that is required. Balloting is rarely necessary and should be conducted only if a motion requiring a ballot was passed before the meeting proceeded to the election of officers.

After the officers have been elected, the acting chair and secretary vacate their places, unless they have been elected to these offices, and the new officers assume their duties.

The next business is the appointment of a committee – a small committee is preferable – to draft by-laws, rules of procedure or other needed regulations that are not embodied in the constitution itself. The chair asks for a motion appointing this committee to be proposed and seconded, and the meeting votes by a show of hands. Usually, the committee that framed the constitution is reappointed for this additional duty, and often this committee is given the authority to draft both a constitution and regulations at the outset. It should be noted, however, that the constitution and the regulations serve different purposes: a constitution states the basic principles underlying an organization's existence; by-laws or other regulations set out the rules and procedures for internal management. It is preferable to leave compiling the by-laws and regulations until after the steps necessary for formal organization have been completed.

After appointing a committee to prepare the rules, the meeting should adjourn to allow the committee to carry out its task, although it can first deal with any urgent, non-controversial items. Controversial matters are best left until after the rules of procedure have been decided, at which point the organization can launch its program.

Procedure at the meeting convened to receive and consider the committee's draft by-laws and regulations is the same as at the meeting held to deal with the constitution. The committee's report, which sets out the draft by-laws or regulations, should be distributed to members in advance of the meeting. This allows members to examine it and facilitates decision making at the meeting. The various proposed items are discussed in order and approved, rejected or amended. When all of them have been considered, a motion should be made and seconded that the report as presented or as amended be adopted. If the motion carries, the by-laws and regulations as adopted are effective until they are further amended. If the committee's report is substantially unacceptable, it can be referred back to the committee for further study

69

and revision, preferably with a statement outlining in what way it is inadequate.

As there are no agreed rules in effect at the meetings at which the constitution and regulations are considered, there should be an understanding that rules commonly observed will apply. The chair can, if necessary, limit debate or otherwise act to ensure that the business of the meeting is conducted equitably and efficiently.

54. Draft Constitution

An organization's constitution is the basis of its existence, its fundamental law. It sets out the organization's name, purpose, the titles and duties of its principal officers, the nature of and qualification for membership, and whatever conditions, limitations or other considerations are needed to establish the organization's essential character. The preparation of the constitution may require expert advice, but many relatively small organizations could adopt the following typical form of constitution after modifying and adapting it to suit individual needs.

The purposes and objectives of the association shall be the encouragement and promotion of studies in Canadian literature. Any profits or other accretions to the association shall be used in the promotion of the aforementioned objects.

The membership of the association shall consist of two classes, namely: (1) active, and (2) honourary.

Active membership shall be open to any resident of this community upon payment of a membership fee in an amount to be determined from time to time at general meetings of the association.

Honourary members shall be elected from among persons in this community who are well known for their interests and activities in the promotion of studies in Canadian literature.

The officers of the association shall be the following: president, first vice-president, second vice-president, secretary and treasurer.

The officers shall be elected at annual meetings of the association to serve for a period of one year.

The officers shall serve as a management (or executive) committee of the association, of which three shall be a quorum. The committee may meet from time to time but not less frequently than once in every calendar month.

Notices of annual and general meetings of the association shall be mailed to each member of record, and/or may be advertised in a local newspaper, not less than four days prior to the date of any such meeting, and shall state the place, date, time and purpose of the meeting.

The annual meeting of the association shall be held in April of each year on a date fixed by the management (or executive) committee. General meetings may be called from time to time as determined by the management (or executive) committee.

The business to be transacted at annual meetings shall be: the consideration and adoption of the minutes of the immediately preceding annual meeting; the consideration of reports of the treasurer and president; the election of officers; the appointment of auditors; and any other business that the management (or executive) committee decides should properly come before the annual meeting.

The presence of not less than twenty members in good standing constitutes a quorum at any general meeting of the association.

A general meeting of the association shall be held within seven days after a request to that effect in writing, signed by not less than twenty members in good standing of the association, is filed with the secretary.

The president shall preside at all meetings of the association and of its management (or executive) committee. In the president's absence, the duties of this office shall be performed by the senior vice-president then present.

Unless otherwise provided, questions arising at any meeting shall be decided by a majority vote of those present. When the votes are equal, but not otherwise, the chair shall have a vote.

If any office becomes vacant, the management (or executive) committee may elect any member in good standing to that office for the unexpired term.

The secretary shall keep a record in minutes of the proceedings of the meetings of the association and the management (or executive) committee. The secretary shall have custody of all books, records and papers of the association, except those in the custody of the treasurer or other person authorized to have possession of them by resolution of the association.

The treasurer shall have supervision of all of the moneys and securities belonging to the association and shall ensure all moneys received are deposited in a chartered bank or credit union to be designated by the management or executive committee. Such moneys shall be withdrawn by cheques signed by the president and the treasurer, but in the absence of either or both of these officers, either of the vice-presidents may act on behalf of the absent officer or officers.

The financial year of the association shall end on the 31st day of March of each year.

The books of the association shall be audited prior to the annual meeting each year by a person or persons as appointed from time to time.

The association may devise and give effect to such by-laws, rules or regulations as may be required for its governance, provided they are consonant with the principles embodied in this constitution.

The constitution of the association may be amended at annual meetings, provided that a notice of motion to amend has been filed with the secretary not less than ten days prior to such annual meeting. An amendment of the constitution shall be effected only with the support of two-thirds of the members voting at the annual meeting.

55. Election of Officers

Associations should set out in their by-laws or regulations the procedures for the election of their officers. The outcome is important and so the method should be fully understood and meticulously observed.

The usual first step is to appoint a nominating committee, whose duty is to ensure that there is a nominee for each elective office. A nominating committee can be appointed by an executive or management committee, or by a general meeting on the latter's recommendation. It should be relatively small, and consist of members who have a knowledge of the association's affairs and who are generally respected and unprejudiced.

The nominating committee should consider the qualities of the individuals eligible for election and should take into account such things as diversities of interest, specific capabilities for performing particular functions, representation in the case of an organization operating over a wide territory or in a multicultural community, and the like. Before making a nomination, the committee must ensure that the proposed nominee is prepared to take the office if elected. A member of the nominating committee can be nominated, although he or she may then feel obliged to withdraw from the nominating committee. As well, the committee can nominate more than one person for a single office. As this will lead to an election for that office, multiple nominations are usually desirable.

Once it has completed its slate of nominees, the nominating committee reports its recommendations to the annual meeting or a meeting called for the election of officers.

Some organizations allow for nominations to be made by any member in writing, accompanied by the signed acceptance of the nominee, provided the nominations are received by a specified date in advance of the meeting at which elections will be held. As well, most organizations allow nominations to be made from the floor at the election meeting, as long as the nominees are present to indicate their willingness to take office if elected, or they have accepted the nomination in writing beforehand. Written nominations or those from the floor are sometimes required to be supported by two or more members as nominators.

If the nominating committee's report is adopted without question and without additional nominations being made, and if it contains only one nominee for each elective office, the nominees promptly declared duly elected by acclamation. In the same circumstances, a motion "That nominations be closed" has, if carried, the same effect.

If there are a number of offices to be filled, the chair of the meeting at which the nominating committee's report is considered should deal

Incorporation can take place by a special act of either the federal or provincial parliaments of Canada, or in some cases under prevailing omnibus acts. More commonly, incorporation takes place under letters patent, and there are special provisions in both the federal and provincial Companies acts for the incorporation of not-for-profit organizations formed to conduct social, philanthropic, scientific, professional and similar operations.

There are formal procedures involved in applying for incorporation, and any organization thinking about taking this step should seek legal advice. An incorporated organization is governed by its corporate charter, which is best drafted with the assistance of a knowledgeable lawyer.

57. Winding Up

Should an association or society decide for any reason to wind up its affairs and bring its organized existence to an end, there is a procedure that should be followed. The decision may stem from a lack of interest, an inability to attain objectives, a lack of funds, or even an extreme personality conflict, but whatever the cause, notice should be given at a general meeting that at the next or a subsequent general meeting a motion will be introduced that the organization be wound up and its effective existence terminated as of a specified date or a date to be fixed. After this motion has been introduced and seconded it is open to debate, and arguments for and against the proposed winding up should be fully aired. To pass, this motion requires the support of not less than two-thirds of those present and qualified to vote, and the chair should inform the members of this requirement before the motion is put to the vote.

At the same meeting, a motion needs to be moved and seconded that authority be given to the management or executive committee, or to a special committee appointed for the purpose, to put the winding up resolution into effect. This entails disposing of whatever assets the organization has in the form either of property, physical goods (ledgers and other books, formal records, furnishings, and so on) or of moneys. Provision has to be made for the safekeeping of records, and it is essential that the members approve a procedure for the disposal of whatever funds there are. These funds belong to the members, so how they are disposed of is decided by them.

Should complications arise in the winding up process, the organization should seek disinterested accounting and/or legal advice and assistance. The winding up of an incorporated body has to comply with statutory procedures; in this case legal services are indispensable.

58. Meetings for Special Purposes
Some types of meetings fall into a rather special category.

The major political parties, for example, have constitutions and codes of procedure that govern the holding of conventions and meetings for the purpose of electing party leaders and nominating candidates for public office, and for framing party programs at the national or provincial levels. The principles of parliamentary law regulate order and decorum at these conventions and meetings, but the mechanisms used by the different branches or party associations, while conforming with an overall pattern, can differ from time to time and place to place. Frequently a special committee is set up to organize these events, devise a program, and provide a procedural outline for the guidance of the presiding officer.

An illustration of this would be a meeting of a local political organization or riding association convened to nominate a candidate for election to the provincial or federal parliament. The executive of the local association will first meet to decide a closing date for the receipt of nominations, the place and date of a nominating meeting, and any other arrangements that need to be made. Usually notice is given, by advertisement or otherwise, that nominations must be filed not later than a specific date, some time ahead of the date of the meeting. The notice should also detail the place, date and time of the meeting, and make it clear that only riding association members in good standing (paid-up by a certain date) will be eligible to vote.

The president of the riding association customarily chairs the nominating meeting. Routine business is disposed of and the chair introduces the main business of nominations. The by-laws of the association may specify the nomination procedures, but if they do not the procedures should be agreed upon at the start of the meeting. It should, for instance, be agreed that voting will be by ballot and that either a plurality or majority vote is required. The meeting should also decide whether the length and number of speeches should be limited, and confirm that parliamentary rules will apply during the debate. Scrutineers, or tellers, of the ballot should be appointed.

If nominations from the floor are acceptable, any member can propose a name, briefly giving reasons for the nomination. If the motion is seconded, the chair then asks whether there are other nominations. If there is only one nomination, any rule requiring a ballot is suspended, and the chair declares the nominee to be the unanimous choice of the meeting.

When there are several nominations, made either in writing prior to the meeting or from the floor, an election must be held. Occasionally a nominee, at some stage in the proceedings, will decline the nomination. To avoid this happening, the nominator should be certain the nominee is willing to stand for election before putting forward his or her name.

The candidates are usually allowed to address the meeting briefly. Then ballots are distributed by the tellers to those entitled to vote, are collected and counted by the tellers when they have been marked, and the result is reported to the chair, who announces it to the meeting.

If, as is common in meetings of this kind, a candidate must receive a majority of the total votes cast in order to win, and if in the first ballot no candidate is given a majority, the name of the candidate receiving the fewest votes on the first ballot is dropped and another ballot is taken on the remaining candidates. The process is repeated until a candidate is elected by an absolute majority of the votes cast.

Another method of balloting is for the secretary or clerk to call the roll of the members or delegates alphabetically, and as each one comes forward, to give each him or her a ballot to mark immediately and return to the secretary for deposit in a box. When everyone has voted, the ballots are counted by the tellers and the result announced in the usual way. While more time-consuming, this procedure has the advantage of recording each vote, avoiding any possibility of error in the distribution and collection of ballots and ensuring secrecy.

Another method of election, the single alternative vote or preferential vote, offers the advantage of determining a majority winner among three or more candidates on a single ballot. Instead of conducting a series of ballots, eliminating one candidate each time until one is given an absolute majority, a single ballot is distributed. The voters do not place a single X opposite one name on the ballot, but indicate their first, second, or third choices, and so on. If there are three candidates A, B and C, a first choice, say A, would be marked 1, a second choice, say C, marked 2, and B marked 3. When the votes are counted, the first-choice votes, the "1" votes, are counted first, and if any candidate receives enough of these to give him or her a clear majority, i.e., one more than half the total number of votes cast, he or she is the winner.

If, however, no candidate secures a majority on the first count, the candidate receiving the fewest "1" votes is eliminated. All the ballots showing that candidate as first choice, and only those ballots, are re-examined and the second-choice votes ("2") are then assigned to the candidates who are still in the running. The process can be repeated, each time eliminating the candidate with the least support and reassigning those votes, until one candidate has a clear majority. This method has the advantage of avoiding multiple balloting, but it does require time and care in the tabulation of the ballots.

At a nomination meeting, the chair and secretary normally have the right to vote with the other delegates, although the chair may decline to do so. The chair should not take part in the discussion after addressing the members at the start of the proceedings. He or she must, however, inform the meeting on points of order, preserve decorum, and otherwise ensure the orderly transaction of the business of the meeting. If improper procedures are used, instead of promptly ruling them out of order, the chair may suggest an alternative means of achieving the desired end.

When an organization wants to state publicly its position or opinion on political, economic or other questions, it usually appoints a committee to draft resolutions or proposals for report to and consideration by a meeting. The report may be dealt with as a whole, but if it contains a number of separate resolutions, each should be individually discussed, adopted, amended or rejected.

Resolutions of this kind do not have to originate in a committee. Most conventions and assemblies will allow proposals properly introduced as motions by individual members either in advance or from the floor, and they are subject to the same procedure of debate, adoption, amendment or rejection. Whether non-committee motions are acceptable is strictly a matter for the organization concerned to decide, provided it is not governed by the rules of a parent organization. In any case, there have to be rules of procedure for the occasion that are consistently applied.

PART IV

Company Meetings

59. General

Generally, under Canadian corporate law, a corporation is treated similarly to a person. Like a person, it has the right to transact business, enter into contracts, hold property, sue and be sued. However, in certain matters the law regards a corporation differently. For example, a corporation can only be fined and not imprisoned for a crime, although, depending upon the circumstance, those in charge of a corporation or responsible for a particular illegal act committed by a corporation may be imprisoned. In addition, while a corporation has the powers of a natural person, its activities may be limited by the charter or other document of incorporation that established it.

Three main types of corporations are recognized under Canadian law: statutory corporations, which are incorporated and governed by a specific statute passed for that purpose (the statute normally including the corporation's governing provisions); charitable and not-for-profit corporations, including clubs, societies and charities, which are governed by boards of directors elected from among their membership; and commercial, share capital corporations, which may be either privately or publicly owned. Commercial corporations raise capital by selling shares to investors or by incurring debt. A public corporation can solicit funds from the public in general and is not restricted in terms of who may invest in it.

Shareholders participate in the fortunes of public corporations through the value of their shares, which can change, and through dividends on shares paid out by the corporation. Shareholders are not personally liable for the corporation's debts and are not involved in directing the ordinary business of the corporation. These matters are administered by the corporation's directors, who are elected by the shareholders, and by its officers, who are appointed by the directors.

In Canada, the federal government, the ten provinces and the two territories each has power to incorporate and govern commercial corporations. The corporate statutes of the thirteen jurisdictions are similar, but there are differences in detail from one to another. The focus of this chapter is on the Canada Business Corporations Act (the CBCA), which applies to commercial corporations incorporated under the federal laws of Canada. Occasionally, this chapter will make specific reference to situations where the CBCA and other statutes impose different requirements. However, as not all instances will be noted, reference should be made to the applicable corporate statute. In general, however, the CBCA's provisions are very similar to the applicable statutes of the other twelve jurisdictions.

Each of the thirteen jurisdictions has the power to establish a commercial company by special statute, including statutes of general application for specific types of corporations such as banks, railways, insurance, trust and loan corporations. As well, each jurisdiction has statutes for the incorporation of co-operatives and condominiums.

Under the CBCA a corporation is created by filing articles of incorporation along with a notice of registered office and a notice of directors in a form prescribed by the act. After a certificate of incorporation is issued, the incorporating directors must convene a meeting to organize the company. At this meeting the incorporating directors must make decisions regarding the implementation of by-laws, the determination of securities, the appointment of officers, auditors and bankers and also consider any other business. The statutes of some of the other jurisdictions require the filing of letters patent, which result in the granting of a charter of incorporation, or the filing of a memorandum of association, which results in the issuance of a certificate of incorporation by the responsible official.

A corporation's articles of incorporation and its by-laws set out the provisions concerning shareholders' meetings and meetings of the board of directors. While all corporations must follow the specific provisions of the relevant jurisdiction's legislation, in general the conduct of meetings differs among corporations according to the terms of the by-laws and the articles of incorporation each has adopted.

60. By-Laws

The by-laws provide the governing framework for the internal management of a corporation. Unless the articles, by-laws or a unanimous shareholders' agreement provide otherwise, the directors are empowered to make, amend or repeal by-laws, subject to approval by the shareholders. Any addition, amendment or withdrawal of a by-law approved by the directors is ineffective if shareholder approval is not subsequently obtained.

As the by-laws must comply with many legislative requirements and play such an important role in the day-to-day operations of a corporation, they should be drafted and reviewed under the guidance of an experienced lawyer. By-laws generally deal with such important matters as the issuance of shares, the qualification and remuneration of directors, the appointment of officers and agents of the company, the declaration and payment of dividends, the time and place for directors' and shareholders' meetings, protection and indemnity for the people acting as officers and directors, and other matters that bear directly on the corporation's policies and procedures.

61. Directors

The shareholders of a corporation elect the directors, normally at the corporation's annual meeting. Under the CBCA, the directors are required to call an annual meeting within eighteen months of the corporation's incorporation date, and thereafter not later than fifteen months following the last annual meeting. Following their election, the directors, who must act and vote as a board of the corporation, are empowered to administer its affairs on behalf of its owners: the shareholders. The board of directors is governed by the articles of incorporation, the by-laws and the applicable corporate statute. Prior to the election of the directors at the initial annual meeting, the directors named in the articles of incorporation as incorporating directors carry out these functions. A director of a commercial corporation under the CBCA and the corporate statutes of most other Canadian jurisdictions, is not required to hold shares in the corporation, unless the articles of incorporation provide otherwise.

Normally, directors are elected annually for a period of one year, and as long as they remain qualified to act as directors, are eligible for re-election. However, in the case of a non-share capital corporation, terms of two or three years are common. If a share capital corporation has not offered its shares to the public, then it may have a board of directors comprised of as few as one person. In the case of a corporation that has offered its shares to the public, and in the case of all non-share capital corporations, the board of directors must be comprised of not fewer than three people. In addition, under the CBCA, the majority of directors of a corporation must be Canadian residents. The act contains an exception for holding corporations, where less than five per cent of the gross revenues of the holding corporation and its subsidiaries is earned in Canada, in which case not more than one-third of the directors need be resident Canadians. The statutes of most other Canadian jurisdictions contain similar provisions regarding the residency of directors. Some jurisdictions require at least one director to be a resident of the particular province (see, for example, British Columbia and Saskatchewan). However, New Brunswick, Nova Scotia and Quebec do not require any directors to be Canadian residents.

Under the Ontario Business Corporation Act, the shareholders may delegate to the board their power to determine the number of directors, subject to the minimum and maximum number provided for in the corporation's articles. However, without shareholder approval, the number of directors may not be increased by more than one-third the number of directors elected at the last annual meeting of the shareholders. Similar provisions exist in Alberta's and British Columbia's corporate legislation. The CBCA does not allow the shareholders to provide the directors with the ability to determine the number of directors.

In order to carry out their functions, the directors meet as a board to make decisions, which are binding upon both the board and the corporation. Before acting independently on behalf of the corporation, a director has to be given specific authority to do so by the board, unless the by-laws provide otherwise. In addition, no director can act or vote by proxy at a meeting of the board of directors. The quorum for a meeting of the board is established either by the articles or the by-laws. Under the CBCA, a quorum is a majority of directors or the minimum number of directors required by the by-laws. However, the articles or by-laws may provide for a smaller quorum. Except for certain holding companies, business may not be transacted at a directors' meeting unless a majority of the directors present at the meeting are resident Canadians. This provision is subject to an exception where a resident Canadian director who is unable to be present approves in writing or by other communication the business transacted at the meeting, and a majority of resident Canadian directors would have been present had that director been present.

The directors may appoint from among themselves a managing director or an executive committee and assign specific functions to that person or committee. Under the CBCA, the managing director must be a resident Canadian, and the executive committee must have a majority of resident Canadians. The directors are also given the power to appoint officers and assign responsibility for the daily operations of the corporation.

In their role as executives in charge of the corporation, the directors have certain duties to the shareholders. In particular, every director of a corporation has a statutory duty to act honestly and in good faith with a view to the best interests of the corporation. Directors must also exercise the care, diligence and skill in carrying out their respective responsibilities within the corporation that a reasonably prudent person would exercise in comparable circumstances.

In this context, it is important to note that the standard of care that applies to directors of non-share capital companies is a common law standard that is subjective in nature. It is not the objective standard set out in the CBCA which applies to directors of commercial corporations. What this means is that the standard of care will differ as it can between two individuals. A director of a non-share capital corporation who has extensive experience or expertise is expected to perform to a higher standard than a director with little experience or expertise. In addition, such directors may be subject to a standard of care that is comparable to that of a trustee.

Directors of public corporations are forbidden from using their inside knowledge of the corporation's affairs to trade their shares for private gain. A director with a personal interest in a matter under consideration by the board must disclose in full what that interest is and usually will be required to abstain from voting on that matter. It has become common practice for a director with a conflict of interest to leave the meeting while the matter is under consideration.

62. Meetings of Directors

The business of the board of directors may be transacted only at a meeting that has been duly called and properly constituted. Under the CBCA, the board of directors may also transact business in writing through resolutions signed by all directors. However, in the case of non-share capital corporations, a meeting must be held. Subject to the provisions of the by-laws, a notice must be given of any meetings to be held. In certain cases the notice must include a description of the matters to be dealt with at the meeting. The chair normally presides at board meetings, or in the chair's absence, the president, a vice-president, or other person appointed by the board. The corporation's by-laws usually deal with the order of precedence for acting as chair.

The rules of procedure for a board meeting are similar to those for an ordinary meeting. An order of business or agenda should always be prepared in advance by the secretary and distributed to the directors. At the meeting, the chair should ensure that the items on the agenda are followed and the secretary that adequate notes are made of the discussions and resolutions of various issues. All decisions concerning significant issues should be made by motion, properly seconded and carried by a majority of the directors. All approved motions should be entered into the minutes of the meeting, which is a permanent record of the decisions taken. In order for a meeting to remain valid, a quorum of directors must be maintained throughout the meeting; any by-law or motion adopted in the absence of a quorum is invalid.

The directors of a newly formed corporation should deal with matters of organization at their first board meeting. Normally these matters would include electing a chair, electing or appointing a secretary and other officers, adopting a common seal, arranging for legal, banking, auditing and other necessary services, appointing a committee to frame the by-laws and other regulations, consideration of where the business of the corporation should be located, consideration of financing issues, and of any other matters necessary to create the operational basis for the corporation.

At their next meeting, the directors should conclude their discussions and decisions on any questions not fully resolved at the initial meeting, and consider any other matters that require attention. Subsequent meetings of the directors will follow a pattern devised to serve the purposes of the corporation. Any business unfinished at an earlier meeting may be brought forward, and time should be allocated for reports from officers or committees that were requested at an earlier meeting. A continuing function of the directors is a review of the corporation's financial position. This includes approving its financial policies, authorizing significant monetary transactions, and taking whatever action is considered necessary regarding the corporation's outstanding shares, subject to applicable statutory limitations.

63. Shareholders' Meetings

All holders of shares in a corporation who are entitled to vote at the shareholders' meeting must receive notice of shareholders' meetings and may participate in and vote at such meetings, unless the share provisions or the articles of incorporation provide otherwise. Under the CBCA, each corporation is required to keep a record of share ownership to ensure that, where notice is required, information concerning the shareholders' eligibility and voting power is available. As previously stated, a corporation must hold its initial annual meeting of shareholders within eighteen months of incorporation and subsequent annual meetings within fifteen months of the last annual meeting. As well, the directors are required by the CBCA to call a special meeting of the shareholders in order to receive approval for any fundamental change to the corporation's affairs requiring an amendment of the articles. At least two-thirds of the shareholders present at a duly constituted shareholders' meeting must approve any such fundamental change. This requirement can also be met through a resolution signed by all the shareholders entitled to vote on the matter. However, this option is not permitted in the case of non-share capital corporations, and a meeting must be held. In addition to other matters, the shareholders of the corporation must approve any additions to, amendments of, or repeals of the corporation's by-laws. While most changes to the by-laws are effective once approved by the directors, in order to remain effective they must be confirmed by the shareholders at their next meeting.

The CBCA also provides for the holders of not less than five per cent of the corporation's voting shares to requisition the directors to convene a special meeting. The requisition must state the business to be transacted at the meeting and must be sent to each director of the corporation. The other jurisdictions also provide this power to shareholders, although some require a greater percentage of shareholders in order to implement a special meeting.

(a) Notice

Notice of a shareholders' meeting must be given in accordance with the applicable corporate legislation and with the corporation's by-laws. Every shareholder entitled to vote at the meeting must be notified of the time and place of the meeting and of the nature of the business to be transacted. Failure to receive notice does not deprive a shareholder of the right to vote at a meeting, provided the shareholder can provide evidence of being a shareholder, if so requested by the corporation. The CBCA requires that notices be forwarded to shareholders not less than twenty-one days and not more than fifty days in advance of the meeting date. The notice period may be different in other jurisdictions.

Notice of a meeting is usually signed by the secretary by order of the board of directors, and it may be accompanied by a proxy form to be completed and returned by a shareholder who is unable to attend the meeting in person. If proxies are being solicited by management, the information that accompanies the proxy form must deal in sufficient detail with the matters to be considered at the meeting that shareholders can make an informed and considered decision. Management is required to solicit proxies under the CBCA when a corporation has fifteen or more shareholders.

Unless the by-laws of the corporation state otherwise, notice of a meeting that has been adjourned for less than thirty days is not required, as it is considered to be the continuation of the original meeting. However, only business left unfinished at the original meeting can be dealt with. If there is new business, notice of the meeting at which it is to be considered must be issued.

(b) Quorum

The by-laws of a corporation normally determine the number of shareholders required to constitute a quorum at a shareholders' meeting. The quorum may be determined either on the basis of the number of shareholders or of the number of shares to be represented at the meeting. A majority of those entitled to vote at a meeting, present in person or by proxy, constitutes a quorum under the CBCA, unless otherwise provided in the by-laws of the corporation. A meeting cannot proceed if there is no quorum available, but the meeting can be adjourned to another fixed time and place. The register of shareholders should always be available to the chair and secretary at any meeting of shareholders' in case a question arises regarding a person's qualification to attend or to be included in the quorum, or if a ballot has to be taken based on share ownership. Similar provisions apply to non-share capital corporations, where members are in an analogous position to shareholders of a commercial corporation.

(c) Proxies

A proxy is the authority to vote given by one person to another. The term is used colloquially both for the document that gives this authorization and for the person who holds it.

Most governing acts or by-laws allow shareholders to be represented at a shareholders' meeting by a proxy. Proxies may be shareholders of the corporation, but do not have to be. An exception to this rule exists for corporations formed under the Nova Scotia Companies Act, where a proxy holder must be a shareholder. A properly executed form of proxy is required in order to be valid, and ordinarily it can be scrutinized by the secretary and its validity ultimately determined by the chair of the meeting. Alternate proxies may be named in a single proxy form. Proxies are effective until validly revoked.

The following is a form of proxy:

The Undersigned, being a holder of (number) shares of (corporation), hereby appoints and authorizes (name of proxy) of the city of (name) to vote for (name of appointer) at the meeting of the corporation to be held (day/month/year) and at any adjournment thereof.

(date and signature of shareholder)

(d) Chairing Meetings

The articles or by-laws of a corporation usually provide that the chair or the president, or in their absences, a vice-president or other officer presides at all shareholder meetings. When there is no such provision, the shareholders may elect the chair from among themselves. The chair has to ensure that proper notice of the meeting has been given and that all the wording of all motions and amendments is in order. The chair is authorized to decide all procedural questions that may arise and that require an immediate decision, and to call for votes and announce results. Unless the meeting otherwise directs, the chair must follow the agenda and call the items of business in order, receive motions and amendments, ensure they are properly seconded, and submit them to the meeting for discussion. The chair must insist that discussion be relevant to the issue under consideration, and that any proposed amendments relate properly to the motions under consideration.

The chair may stop discussion of any question that in the chair's opinion has been fully debated and call for a vote on the motion. When all items of business on the agenda are completed, the chair asks whether there is any other business to be considered and rules whether any such new business is in order. When all the business is completed, the chair closes or terminates the meeting.

(e) Procedure

When the chair is satisfied a quorum is present, he or she calls the meeting to order. The secretary then reads the notice calling the meeting and certifies that it has been mailed to the shareholders in accordance with the governing corporate legislation. Scrutineers may be appointed to verify the number of shareholders represented in person or by proxy. The minutes of the last meeting are normally approved and, if necessary, corrected and signed by the chair. The business of the meeting is then dealt with in the order in which the various items appear on the agenda, unless otherwise agreed to at the meeting. The items covered at an annual meeting of shareholders include the presentation of financial statements and auditors' report, the election of directors and the appointment of auditors. In addition, directors often present a formal report to the shareholders, which is accompanied by a statement by the president of the corporation on the corporation's current operating position. Such reports are normally not subject to formal approval by the shareholders.

Any proposals introduced for the shareholders' approval should be in written form and should be presented with a motion for adoption. Most motions can be debated and amended in accordance with normal practice. However, if a proposal is introduced on a matter of substance in specific terms, and the shareholders have been previously informed of these terms, it should be presented only as disclosed to shareholders and either approved or rejected without amendment. The only permissible amendment in these circumstances would be the adoption of wording to clarify, without altering, the intent of the motion. The inclusion of substantial new items, without prior notice to shareholders, is considered unfair to shareholders present at the meeting in person and, especially, to those represented by proxy or not represented at all.

The chair has no authority to conclude or adjourn a meeting before the business set down for consideration has been completed, unless there is a provision in the by-laws or articles empowering the chair to do so.

(f) Voting

The by-laws of every corporation should include regulations regarding the voting at shareholders' meetings. In addition, the share provisions attached to the various classes of shares outstanding in the capital of the corporation will determine whether the holders of such shares are entitled to vote, and the number of votes attached to such shares.

Where a corporation has only one class of shares, the CBCA provides that shareholders are entitled to vote at each meeting of shareholders. Votes may be cast in person or by proxy. All motions are decided by a majority vote, and all special motions require the approval of at least two-thirds of the votes cast at a duly called meeting. As previously discussed, under the CBCA, written motions signed by all shareholders eligible to vote on a matter fulfil the shareholder approval requirement.

It is important to note that in cases where the shareholders of a corporation are subject to a "unanimous shareholders' agreement," the agreement may affect the voting procedure. See Section 146 of the CBCA in this regard.

Ordinarily, shareholders vote by a show of hands without regard for the number of shares held. Any shareholder may demand a ballot, however, and unless the procedure for a ballot is set out in the corporation's by-laws, the chair decides how it is to be conducted. Issues of substance should always be decided by ballot, as the decision should be based upon majority share representation.

A shareholder can demand a ballot on any question under consideration even if a vote has already been held by a show of hands. It may be expedient to conduct the ballot immediately or at the conclusion of the meeting when all other business has been transacted. In conducting the vote, shareholders are supplied with a ballot paper which they mark either for or against the motions under consideration and then sign. Scrutineers appointed before the vote then note on each ballot the number of shares held in person or represented by proxy by the person signing the ballot. The votes for and against are totalled after all the ballots have been cast (there being one vote per share or as otherwise specified in the articles of the corporation). The scrutineers then report their findings to the chair, who announces the results. The by-laws of the corporation may provide the chair with a second or casting vote in the case of a tie.

64. Minutes
The CBCA requires that every corporation record minutes of all meetings of shareholders, directors and any executive committees. Such minutes should be retained in the corporate minutes book, along with the by-laws of the corporation. Minutes should also be kept of all meetings of all committees of the board and submitted to the full board for its information and comment at the first board meeting following the committee meeting. It is normally the responsibility of the secretary of the corporation to record the minutes while the meeting is in progress,

under the direction of the chair, and to prepare a fair copy as soon as possible afterward. The minutes are normally submitted for approval at the next meeting of the relevant group. The minutes should be indexed in the minutes books so that they can be referred to easily.

The minutes should record the place, date and time of the meeting and show that all governing acts and by-laws, including notice, have been complied with. The chair and secretary should be named, and those in attendance listed, at least to the extent of showing that a quorum was present. For a shareholders' meeting, the number of shares represented in person and those represented by proxy should be recorded. The minutes should contain the full text of every motion and amendment considered and state whether it was adopted or rejected. The names of proposers and seconders of motions, and of those who voted for and against, do not have to be recorded, but any member can request that his or her vote against a motion be recorded, and the secretary should comply. Reports or other documents presented at a meeting can be incorporated in the minutes as an appendix, and reference to them made in the body of the minutes themselves. The details of contracts or other matters involving finances should be fully recorded in the minutes.

65. Company Books and Records

Under the CBCA, corporations are required to maintain certain books and records. These include:

1. the articles of incorporation, and any amendments thereto;
2. all by-laws of the corporation;
3. a copy of any unanimous shareholders' agreement known to the directors;
4. the minutes of meetings and resolutions of the shareholders;
5. a register of directors, setting out the names and residential addresses, and the dates on which each director became or ceased to be a director;
6. an alphabetical listing of all shareholders of the corporation including the name, address and number and class of shares held by such shareholder;
7. adequate accounting records; and

8. records containing minutes of meetings or resolutions of the directors and of any committee of the board.

The books and records of a corporation are normally kept at the head office of the corporation, or at its registered office or at another place in Canada designated by the directors. The books and records must be open to examination by any director at all reasonable times, and certain corporate records must also be available for review by shareholders and creditors of the corporation during normal business hours. The shareholders' and creditors' duly appointed agents and legal representatives have the same right of access to a corporation's records.

PART V

Some Illustrations

(In the following illustrations, it is assumed that the meeting is being chaired by a woman and that the secretary is a man.)

Suspension of Rules

Chair: Will the meeting please come to order? Ladies and gentlemen [or Friends], as you are aware, this meeting has been called somewhat hurriedly, as we face a deadline. It was not possible to give the required ten days' notice of the meeting, as specified in our by-laws, and so our first action must be to suspend, for the purposes of this meeting only, that requirement of our by-laws.

Member A: I move that, for the purposes of this meeting only, the ten-day notice requirement be suspended.

Member B: Second.

Chair: Is anyone opposed? No. I therefore declare this meeting duly called and regularly constituted.

Minutes

Chair: The first order of business is the confirmation of minutes. Mr. Secretary, will you please read the minutes of the last meeting.

(The secretary does so.)

Chair: Are the minutes in order? If so, may I have a motion for their adoption?

Member C: Madam Chair, I believe there is one error. Mr. A. was named a member of the nominating committee but in the minutes his name is not included with the other committee members.

Chair: Thank you. Does anyone disagree? Mr. Secretary, please make that correction.

With that correction, are the minutes now in order?

Member D: I move that the minutes of the last meeting as corrected be approved and confirmed.

Member E: Second.

Chair: All in favour? Thank you. The next order of business is . . .

Report of Committee

. . . a report from our finance committee. Ms. B., as chair of that committee, please submit your report.

(Ms. B. does so.)

Chair: You have now heard the report. Is there any comment?

Alternative I

Member A: I move that the report of the finance committee be received.

Chair: If there is no further comment . . . (pause) . . . the report is received and it will be filed in our records.

Alternative II

Member A: Madam Chair, in my view there is some confusion of the data contained in Part 2 of the report. May I suggest that instead of . . . (explains the point).

Chair: Do you agree, Ms. B?

(There is discussion of the point.)

Chair: We seem to be agreed that this clarification is needed. Would the report revised as suggested be acceptable?

Member B: I move that the report of the finance committee, as revised, be adopted.

Member C: I second the motion.

Chair: It has been moved and seconded that the report of the finance committee, as revised, be adopted. All in favour? . . . Are any opposed? . . . Thank you. The motion carries.

Alternative III

Member A: Madam Chair, in my view Part 2 of the report is very confusing and the data it contains are inadequate to support the conclusions reached. Is it in order to ask the committee to amplify this part of its report and resubmit it to our next meeting?

Chair: Your proposal is in order provided it is supported by other members. What is the opinion of the meeting?

Member B: Madam Chair, I agree. I move that the finance committee's report be referred back to the committee for substantial amplification of Part 2 and resubmission at our next meeting.

Member C: I second the motion.

Chair: It has been moved and seconded that the report of the finance committee be referred back to the committee for substantial amplification of Part 2 and resubmission at our next meeting. Is there any discussion? . . . (there is none) . . . Those in favour of the motion? . . . Those opposed? . . . The motion carries. I therefore request the finance committee to act on the motion. The resubmission of their report will be an item on the agenda of our next meeting.

Electing a Chair of a Meeting Called for a Special Purpose

One of the convenors: Ladies and gentlemen, will you please come to order? As you know, this meeting of interested persons has been called for the sole and express purpose of deciding whether we should appoint a delegation to approach our municipal council on the question of . . . (briefly describes the issue). In order to constitute this meeting properly, we should elect a chair and secretary. May I have nominations, please?

Voice 1: I nominate Ms. A. as chair.

Voice 2: I nominate Mr. B. as chair.

Convenor: Are there other nominations? . . . (There are none) . . . Then I would ask you to vote on the two nominations in the order in which they are made. Will those in favour of Ms. A. as chair please raise their right hand. . . . Those opposed? . . . The vote is against Ms. A. The second nominee is Mr. B. Will those in favour of Mr. B. as chair please raise their hands. . . . Those opposed? . . . I declare Mr. B. duly elected as chair of this meeting.

(An identical procedure is then followed for the election of a secretary or any other officer required for the purposes of the meeting.)

Electing a Chair of a Formative Meeting

One of the convenors: Friends, as you know, our purpose this evening is to consider whether to establish an on-going organization to be concerned with (describes purposes). Our first order of business must be the election of a chair and secretary to serve during our preliminary discussions and until such time as we may decide to form a permanent organization with a constitution and by-laws providing for regular elections. May I have nominations, please?

(The procedure is then identical to that in the preceding example.)

Choosing a Chair in the Absence of Regular Presiding Officers

Secretary: Friends, both our president and vice-president are unavoidably absent today and they have asked me to convey their apologies. Would you please therefore appoint a chair *pro tem.* for the purposes of this meeting?

Member: I nominate Ms. A. to act as chair *pro tem.*

(Such a nomination is usually found acceptable by the members, in which case no further action is necessary and Ms. A. takes the chair. Should another nomination or other nominations be made, election procedures are the same as in the previous examples.)

Quorum

Chair: Friends, it is now twenty minutes past the hour. We do not have, and it does not appear that we will have, a quorum. I regret that this means we cannot proceed with our meeting. Thank you for coming. Our next meeting will be our regular monthly meeting, and due notice of it will be sent to you. The items on today's agenda will appear on the agenda of our next meeting, together with any new business that may develop in the interim.

Alternative

Chair: Friends, we have lost quorum and so we cannot make any further decisions regarding our association's business. I suggest that instead we discuss informally the remaining items on our agenda, but I should point out to you that we can come to no conclusions nor take any action concerning them. The items will appear on the agenda of our next meeting. Is this procedure acceptable?

Motions

Chair: The next order of business is the proposed submission of a brief by this association to the Commission on Energy Resources.

Member A: Madam Chair, I think this is outside our usual sphere of interest. I move that we take no action in the matter.

Chair: Is there a seconder for this motion?

(There is no seconder.)

Chair: This motion is not seconded and so we cannot deal with it.

Member B: I believe that we have something to say in this matter, Madam Chair. I move that a brief be prepared and that it be submitted to the commission on our behalf.

Member C: I second that motion.

Chair: It has been moved and seconded that a brief be prepared and submitted to the Commission on Energy Resources on behalf of our association. The matter is open for discussion.

(Debate follows.)

Member D: Madam Chair, it is obvious that it will take a lot of work to prepare this brief. I move to amend the motion by providing that a special committee be appointed by the chair to study the whole matter and prepare a draft brief for our approval.

Member E: I second the motion to amend.

Chair: You have heard the proposed amendment. Is there any comment?

(The proposed amendment is discussed.)

Member F: Madam Chair, we don't have much time before we have to submit this brief to the commission. Therefore, I move a subamendment that the committee submit its draft brief for our approval at our next regular monthly meeting.

Member G: Second.

Chair: You have heard the subamendment. Is there further discussion?

(There is none.)

Chair: The question is as follows: It is moved that a brief be prepared and submitted to the Commission on Energy Resources on behalf of our association; by amendment it is moved that a committee be appointed by the chair to study the whole question and prepare a draft brief for our approval; by subamendment it is moved that the draft brief be submitted for our approval at our next monthly meeting.

Member H: Madam Chair, I move that we contract the services of an expert to help us prepare our brief.

Chair: Mr. H, we have before us a main motion, an amendment and a subadmendment. At this point your motion is not in order.

I shall now put the question. Those in favour of the subamendment please raise your hands. (There is a show of hands.) Those opposed? (There are none.) All those in favour of the amendment as amended, please raise your hands. (Again a show of hands and none opposed.) Those in favour of the main motion as amended? (A show of hands.) Opposed? (One hand rises, indicating that there is one opponent of the principle embodied in the main motion.) The motion carries.

Member A: Madam Chair, I should like my negative vote to be recorded.

Chair: Mr. Secretary, please record Ms. A.'s negative vote in the minutes.

Postponement of Action on Motion

(In the following examples a main motion is before the meeting and debate is in progress.)

Alternative I

Member A: (after gaining the chair's attention) Madam Chair, I move that the debate be adjourned.

Chair: Is there a seconder for the motion that the debate be adjourned?

Member B: I second the motion.

Member C: Madam Chair, I object. It seems to me that . . .

Chair: Mr. C, I am sorry, but you are out of order. A motion to adjourn is not debatable. It has been moved and seconded that the debate on the motion that (states the main motion) be adjourned. All in favour? . . . Those opposed? . . . The motion carries. The next order of business is . . .

(If the motion to adjourn is defeated, the debate on the main motion continues as though there had been no intervention.)

Alternative II

Member A: Madam Chair, I move that we proceed to the next order of business.

Member B: I second the motion.

Chair: It has been moved and seconded that we proceed to the next

100

order of business. Those in favour? . . . Those opposed? . . . The motion is lost. Debate will proceed on the main motion before us, which is . . .

(If the motion had carried, the chair would have at once proceeded to the next item on the agenda. The suspended motion could, however, be revived at a subsequent meeting.)

Alternative III ("the previous question")

Member A: Madam Chair, I move that the question be now put.

Member B: I second the motion.

Chair: It has been moved and seconded that the question be now put. Is there any discussion?

(The motion is debatable, but debate is restricted to this motion; the main motion to which it refers is not debatable at this point.)

Chair: Does the meeting wish the question to be now put? Those in favour? . . . Those opposed? . . . The motion carries. I shall now put the question (the main motion) which is as follows . . .

OR

The motion is lost and so the question may *not* be now put. The next order of business is . . .

(Again, a question set aside in this way may be reintroduced at a subsequent meeting.)

Alternative IV

Member A: Madam Chair, in my view this question demands much more investigation than we can give it this evening. I therefore move that we refer it to our committee on procedures for study and report.

Member B: I second the motion.

Chair: It has been moved and seconded that the meeting refer the question before us, namely (briefly states the question), to our committee on procedure for study and report. Is there any discussion?

Member C: Yes, Madam Chair. In view of the monetary considerations involved, I move to amend the motion to refer by adding the words "in consultation with the finance committee" after the words "committee on procedure."

Member D: I second the motion to amend.

Chair: It has been moved and seconded to amend the motion to refer by adding the words "in consultation with the finance committee." Is there any discussion of the proposed amendment? . . . No. Will those in favour of the amendment please raise their hands. . . . Those opposed? . . . The amendment carries. The motion to refer as amended is now as follows: (states the motion). Is there any further discussion? . . . Those in favour? . . . Opposed? . . . The motion carries. The question before us, namely that (states *main* motion), is therefore referred. The next order of business is . . .

Notice of Motion

. . . a notice of motion to amend the by-laws of our association. Mr. A, please.

Mr. A: Yes, Madam Chair. I give notice that at the next or a subsequent meeting I will introduce a motion to amend the by-laws of the association as follows: (he can either provide full details of the amendment he will propose or merely summarize its intent on the understanding that members will be supplied with full details prior to the meeting at which it will be considered.)

Member B: Madam Chair, it seems to me that the change in the by-laws suggested will be counter-productive. It will . . .

Chair: Ms. B, discussion at this stage is not in order. There will be full opportunity to debate the proposed changes when the motion to amend the by-laws is introduced. The next order of business is . . .

Order

(A motion is before the meeting and debate is in progress.)

Member A: (interrupting speaker) Madam Chair, on a point of order, the member is not addressing the question under consideration; she is talking about another subject, which is a separate item later in today's agenda.

Chair: Your point is well taken, Mr. A. Ms. B, please confine your remarks to the question before us, which is . . . (states gist of motion).
  OR
Chair: I disagree, Mr. A. In my view Ms. B's remarks are relevant to the question under discussion, and I so rule.

Member A: I appeal the ruling of the chair.

Member C: I second the appeal.

Chair: The chair's ruling regarding the relevancy of Ms. B's remarks is appealed. Should the chair's ruling be sustained? Those in favour? . . .

Those opposed? . . . The ruling of the chair is sustained. Please continue, Ms. B.

(Should the ruling not be sustained, the chair must ask Ms. B to confine her remarks strictly to the question, and must see that she does so, repeatedly admonishing her if necessary.)

Ms. B: I resent these repeated interruptions . . . (uses intemperate language).

Chair: Order, please.

Ms. B: I will not be dictated to by . . . (more intemperate language).

Chair: Order, please. Ms. B, I must ask you to refrain from these outbursts and follow the rules for this meeting. If you refuse to do so I must ask you to resume your seat, and I shall call upon another speaker.

(The meeting proceeds, but is later distracted by conversations between members.)

Chair: Excuse me, Ms. B. Order, please. Order. Please give the speaker the courtesy of your attention. If anyone has a point of privilege or a point of order to raise, please address your point to the chair. No other interruptions will be tolerated. Please proceed, Ms. B.

(Repeated efforts to maintain order fail.)

Chair: Ladies and gentlemen, this meeting cannot proceed without order and we do not now have order. I shall therefore recess the meeting for twenty minutes. We shall reconvene at (states time) and resume our discussion at the point at which it was broken off.

Privilege

(Debate is in progress.)

Member: (interrupts speaker) Madam Chair, I rise on a point of privilege. Ms. B has attributed to me remarks that I did not, in fact, make, implying . . . (explains his point).

Chair: Ms. B, you have heard Mr. A's point. I think we should pause for a moment for clarification.

(Mr. A establishes that he did not make the remarks attributed to him, and Ms. B apologizes for her misunderstanding.)

Chair: Does that clear your point, Mr. A?

Mr. A: Yes, Madam Chair, thank you.

Chair: Ms. B, please proceed.

Form of Minutes

Minutes of a meeting of the Multicultural Society held at the Ukrainian Hall, Brandon, Manitoba, on Wednesday, 10 March 1995, called to order at 2:30 p.m.

Present: Alice Chan, Duncan Edwards, Henry Fortunato, Isaac Krieger, Michelle Lalonde, Elaine Nowakowski, Frank Quayle, Amarjit Singh, Timothy Vernon, William Yee.

Also attending by invitation: Andrew Krizalkovic and Doris Leung. The president, Ms. Chan, in the chair.

The chair introduced and welcomed Mr. Krizalkovic and Ms. Leung, who were attending as representatives of the Winnipeg branch.

Minutes

The minutes of the last meeting, held 11 February 1995, were read and confirmed on motion.

Correspondence

Receipt was reported of the following communications:

(a) From the Daily Advertiser, dated 25 February 1995, quoting rates in response to the Society's request.

(b) From Mr. Hasan Ramos, dated 16 February 1995, submitting his resignation due to his transfer to a new post in Halifax.

It was agreed: re (a) to refer the matter of an advertising program to the executive committee for consideration and report; re (b) to accept the resignation with regret.

Relations with Winnipeg Branch

At the chair's request Mr. Krizalkovic and Ms. Leung described the recent activities of the Winnipeg branch, with particular reference to representations recently made to the Ministry of Health in the matter of community health clinics. The representations had not led to a satisfactory outcome. They suggested a new, joint approach by representatives of the society's various branches across Manitoba to make a more forceful presentation.

The matter was discussed at some length before it was unanimously agreed, on motion duly seconded, that representatives of each of the society's five branches should be requested to meet to determine a program of concerted action.

The chair was authorized to take such action as might be necessary to put this decision into effect.

The chair thanked Mr. Krizalkovic and Ms. Leung for their attendance, and they withdrew.

Financial Report

A report of the finance committee for the period ended 29 February 1995 was received and approved. (Copy attached.)

Concern was expressed over the increasing gap between revenues and expenditures, and an improved effort to recover dues now in arrears was advocated.

Proposed Submission to Commission on Learning

The chair introduced the question of a proposed submission by this society to the Commission on Learning, and it was duly moved that a brief be prepared and submitted.

In the course of debate an amendment was offered that a special committee be appointed by the chair to study the whole matter and prepare a draft brief for approval. In further debate a subamendment was offered that the committee submit the proposed draft brief for approval at the society's next monthly meeting.

The questions being put and the amendments carried, the motion as amended was adopted. It was thereby resolved:

> That a brief be prepared and submitted on the society's behalf to the Commission on Learning; that a committee be appointed by the chair to study the whole matter and prepare a draft brief for approval, and that the draft brief in question be submitted for approval not later than the society's next monthly meeting.

One member, William Yee, dissented from the decision.

Annual Meeting

The chair reported that in conformity with the provisions of the by-laws the society's annual meeting would be held in the month of May. Suitable arrangements for the meeting were being made by the executive committee, with a tentative date of Thursday, May 27. Notification would be sent by mail to all members.

There being no further business, the chair closed the meeting.

Minutes confirmed ——— Secretary ———

Form of Report

Pursuant to a resolution adopted at a meeting of the society held 10 March 1995, the following were appointed as a committee to prepare a draft brief for submission to the Commission on Learning: Isaac Krieger, Elaine Nowakowski, Amarjit Singh (chair), and the president *ex officio*. The committee has met on a number of occasions. It has examined the terms of reference of the Commission on Learning and has reviewed the relevant policies of our society. It is the committee's opinion that . . . (general statement of relevant considerations, etc.) The committee therefore recommends:

(a) That a brief in the terms of the draft attached to this report be submitted to the Commission on Learning.

(b) That the submission be made by the president of the society, accompanied by such other members as she may name, at a time and place to be arranged.

(c) That copies of the brief be released to the news media immediately following its formal submission.

(signed) Amarjit Singh

chair

(If the report is adopted at the general meeting without change, each of its recommendations must be acted upon. It and the accompanying draft brief are, however, subject to revision at the general meeting and what final action will be taken is determined on the basis of the revisions. All revisions should be explicitly recorded in the minutes.)

Form of Minutes for Board of Directors

Epsilon Company Limited

Meeting of board of directors held at the company's head office, 111 King Street West, Toronto, on Monday, 9 February 1995, at 10:30 a.m.

Present: directors Allan Brown, Catherine Evans, Frank Nemeth.

Leave of Absence: Stephen Jacobi and Peter Raven. Also attending: the general manager, Noah Oates, and secretary, Barbara Moon.

Ms. Catherine Evans, president, in the chair.

Notice

Proof of service of notice of meeting was filed by the secretary.

Minutes

The minutes of the last meeting of the directors, held 5 January 1995, were read and approved and were ordered to be signed as correct.

Statement of Finances

A statement of finances for the six-month period ended 31 December 1994 was reviewed and approved.

Contract with Gamma Corporation

A draft contract with Gamma Corporation was reviewed and, subject to minor adjustment, its execution by the president was authorized on motion.

Correspondence from Delta Associates

A letter addressed to the company by Delta Associates, dated 31 January 1995, was read. The directors being of the opinion that . . . etc., the secretary was directed to reply accordingly.

Annual Meeting

To comply with the provisions of the by-laws it was, on motion duly seconded, unanimously resolved:

> That the annual meeting of shareholders of the company be held at the head office of the company on Wednesday, 31 March 1995, at 2:30 p.m.

There being no further business, the meeting terminated.

Minutes confirmed———   President———
                                      Secretary———

Form of Minutes for Shareholders' Meeting

Minutes of a special general meeting of the shareholders of the Epsilon Company Limited held at the head office of the company, 111 King Street West, Toronto, on Tuesday, 15 June 1995, at 2:30 p.m. Present: Allan Brown, Catherine Evans, Frank Nemeth, Barbara Moon and Noah Oates . . . (and others).

Ms. Catherine Evans, president, in the chair.

Scrutineers

The chair appointed Norman Percy, Virginia Rance and Shyam Umial as scrutineers to report on the number of shares represented and on any poll taken at this meeting.

Quorum

A quorum of the shareholders, in person and by proxy, having been found by the scrutineers, the chair declared the meeting validly constituted.

Notice

The notice convening the meeting was read by the secretary, who filed with the chair a certificate proving mailing of notice to the shareholders. The certificate was ordered appended to the minutes of this day's meeting.

Minutes

The minutes of the special general meeting held 12 May 1994 were read by the secretary and were approved on motion.

Report of Directors

It was resolved unanimously that the report of the directors and the accounts annexed thereto, having been distributed, be taken as read, and upon motion duly seconded it was resolved that such report and accounts be, and they are hereby, adopted.

Election of Director

Upon motion duly seconded and carried unanimously Mr. Arthur B. Currie was elected to the board of directors in the place of Mr. Frank Nemeth, retired.

Administrative Policy

It was moved by Mr. Bennett, seconded by Ms. Phillips:

> That . . . (the actual terms of a specific motion relating to administrative policy, details of which have been supplied to the shareholders in advance of the meeting).

It was moved in amendment by Ms. Archer seconded by Mr. Cozza:

> That the action proposed be deferred pending the appointment of a committee of five shareholders, with power to add to their number, to enquire into the administrative structure and management experience of the company, such committee being authorized to call for books and documents and to obtain such legal and other assistance as may be necessary and to report to a special general meeting of shareholders to be held not later than 31 January 1996.

On a show of hands, the chair declared the amendment lost. A poll was then demanded and taken and showed——— votes for the amendment and ——— votes opposed. (A report of the scrutineers, if any, may be entered in the minutes.) The chair declared the amending motion lost. The question then being put on the main motion, it was resolved in the affirmative.

There being no further business, the chair declared the meeting terminated.

Minutes confirmed———   President———

                                               Secretary———

Index

Abstention, 13

Acclamation, election by, 13, 73-74

Actionable remarks *see* Privilege

Adjournment, 13, 25-26, 50-51, 58, 91, 100; *see also* Closing a meeting

Administration Services of the House of Commons, 21

Advertisements for meetings *see* Notice of meetings

Agenda, 13, 43, 46; *see also* Order of business

Annual meetings, of corporations, 83

Apologies, 29

Appealing a ruling, 28, 53, 102

Appropriation bills *see* Supply bills

Assemblies, lawful and unlawful, 64-65

Assets, disposing of an association's, 76-77

Associations: forming, 67-76; winding up, 76-77

Attendance, 21

Ballot, voting by, 13, 55, 66, 69, 74-75, 78-79, 92; *see also* Voting

Banks, 82

Bentham, Jeremy, 10

Bill of Rights *see* Charter of Rights and Freedoms

Bills: private, 36-37; private members', 37-38; public, 34; supply, 16, 31, 34-35; tax, 17, 34

Board of Internal Economy, 20

Board of Directors *see* Directors

Books *see* Records, company

Bourinot, Sir John George, 11

Budget, presentation of, 17

Business Corporations Act *see* Canada Business Corporations Act

By-laws, 14, 39, 44-45, 50, 69, 88; of a corporation, 82-83

Cabinet ministers *see* Ministers

Call to order, 15

Canada Gazette, 37

Canada Business Corporations Act, 11-12, 82-89, 91-93

Canada Communications Group, 18

Casting vote, 14, 27, 55

Certificate of incorporation, 82

Chair, duties of, 53-54, 56-59, 63, 65, 68, 75, 79, 90-91; electing, 97-98; request to leave, 43; voting rights of, 55; *see also* Presiding officer

Charitable corporations, 81

Charter: of an association, 39; corporate, 76, 82

Charter of Rights and Freedoms, 64

Churchill, Winston, 11

Clerk-at-the-Table, 27

Clerk of Petitions, 33

Clerk of the House, 20-21, 34

Closing a meeting, 57-58, 67, 91; *see also* Adjournment

Closure, 14, 26

Clubs, 81

Co-operatives, incorporating, 82

Commercial corporations, 81

Committal, 52

Committee of the whole, 14, 31-32, 60, 62

Committees, 60-61, 67-69; executive, 61; legislative, 33, 35; nominating, 72-74; reports of,

111

96-97; special, 33, 60; standing, 32-33, 35-36, 60; striking, 32; *see also* Committee of the whole

Companies acts, 76

Company meetings, 81-94

Condominiums, incorporating, 82

Conflict of interest, 85-86

Constitution Act, 10, 19

Constitution of an association, 14, 39, 44, 49-50, 68-69; sample, 70-72

Corporations, 81

Counsel, Legislative, 37

Debate, 22, 24-25, 52-53; adjourning, 32; limiting, 26, 53

Debts, corporate, 82

Decorum, breach of, *see* Disturbances, Inappropriate language

Deferment, 51-52; *see also* Postponements

Deputy Clerk, 21

Deputy Speaker, 20, 37

Dilatory motions, 15, 25-26, 50

Directors, corporate, 82-87; register of, 93

Discipline, 29-30, 56-57; *see also* Disturbances, Inappropriate language

Disturbances, handling, 29, 56, 58, 66, 103

Division, 14, 27

Elections *see* Ballot, Voting

Emergency debates, 25

Ending a meeting *see* Adjournment, Closing a meeting

Enumeration, 55

Ex officio, 14

Executive committees, 61

Expenditures, government, 31

Financial statements, 59

Formality, in meetings, 62-63

Freedom: of speech, 11, 64; of association, 64

Funds, disposing of an association's, 76-77

Government House Leader, 30

Governor General, 36

Hansard, 38

Heckling *see* Disturbances

Holding companies, 84-85

Illegal meetings *see* Unlawful assemblies

Inappropriate language, 20, 29, 103

Incorporation, 75-76, 82

Informality, in meetings, 63, 67

Insider trading, 85-86

Insurance companies, 82

Journals, legislative, 22, 38

Legal action *see* Libel, Privilege, Slander

Legislative Committees, 33, 35

Legislative Counsel, 37

Letters patent, 76, 82

Liability, of shareholders, 82

Libel, 57

Loan companies, 82

Mace, 21

Magna Carta, 9

Mail ballots, 55

Majority vote, 14, 55, 75, 78

Managing director, 85

Mayor, 42

Meetings, 40-41; notice of, 41; preliminary, 67-69

Members of Parliament, 28-30

Membership in organizations, 39

Memorandum of association,
   82
Ministers, cabinet, 26, 30, 35-36
Minority reports, 62
Minutes, 46, 58-59, 62, 90, 95-96; of
   shareholders' meetings, 92-93;
   samples, 104-9
Misquotation, 24
Motions, 14, 20, 22-26, 46-52, 67,
   99-102; dilatory, 15, 25-26, 50;
   notice of, 49-50, 102; privileged,
   22; recording, 93; rescinding, 22,
   47-48; speaking to, 24; special,
   25-26; subsidiary, 15; substantive,
   14, 22
Mover, 15
Municipal councils, 40, 41

Nominating committees, 72-74
Nominations, 97-98; of officers, 68,
   73-74; of political candidates,
   77-78; of presiding officer, 44
Non-profit corporations, 81
Non-share capital corporations,
   84-87, 89
Notice: of meetings, 41, 65, 86, 88;
   of motion, 49-50, 102
Nova Scotia Companies Act, 89

Objections, 55
Offensive remarks *see* Inappropriate
   language
Officers, 15; election of, 68-69,
   72-75; corporate, 85; of the House
   of Commons, 20-21
Ontario Business Corporation Act,
   84
Order, 15; breach of, 53, 56; points
   of, 24, 28, 31, 56, 102-3; of
   business, 21-22, 46, *see also*
   Agenda
Order Paper, 15, 21, 30, 34, 36-38
Orders of the day, 15, 25

Parliament: convening, 19; sittings
   of, 41
Parliamentary privilege, 28
Parties, political, 77
Peace, disturbing the, 64
Petitions, 33-34
Plurality, 15, 75
Points of order *see* Order, points of
Political parties, 77
Poll *see* Ballots, Voting
Postponements, 25, 51-52, 100; *see
   also* Deferment
Presiding officer, 42-45; *see also*
   Chair, Speaker
Previous question, 26, 51, 52, 101
Private bills, 36-37
Private members' bills, 37
Private members' business, 21
Privilege, 16, 19, 28-29, 57, 103
Privy Council Office, 34
Pro tem., defined, 16
Propriety, 53; *see also* Inappropriate
   language
Proxies, 85, 88-90
Public bills, 34
Public corporations, 81
Public meetings, 65-67
Publicity, principle of, 10
Putting the question *see* Question

Question Period, 30
Question, putting the, 16, 26-27,
   51-54, 100
Questions: supplementary, 30; of
   order *see* Order, points of
Quorum, 16, 21, 33, 45, 58, 61,
   85-86, 89, 98

Railway companies, 82
Recess, 56, 58, 103
Reconsideration, 48
Records, association, 58-59, 76;
   company, 93-94

Reeve, 42
Reference, 16, 52
Regulations, of an association, 69-70
Relevancy, 53, 67
Reports: committee, 61-62, 74, 96-97; minority, 62; Parliamentary, 38; samples, 106
Resolutions, 16, 22, 79
Riding associations, 77-78
Right of assembly, 64
Rights, violation of, 57
Royal Assent, 36
Rules: creating, 39; suspending, 40, 95; *see also* Regulations
Rulings, appealing, 28, 53, 102

Scrutineers, 16, 75, 78, 90, 92; *see also* Tellers
Seal, of a corporation, 86
Second reading, 31
Seconding, 16, 24, 47
Secretary, duties of, 46, 65, 58-59, 78, 86, 90, 92-93
Senate, 32, 36
Sergeant-at-Arms, 21
Session, 41
Share capital corporations, 81
Shareholders, 81-84; meetings, 87-93; register of, 89, 93
Shares, issuing, 83
Signing officer, 44
Slander, 57
Speaker, Deputy, 20, 31
Speaker, 10, 42; duties of, 19-38; election of, 19
Speaking to a motion, 24
Special committees, 33, 60
Special-purpose meetings, 77
Standing Committee on Procedure and House Affairs, 29, 32-33, 37-38
Standing committees, 32-33, 35, 36, 60

Standing Orders of the House, 11, 18-38
Standing vote, 54-55
Statutes, 39
Statutory corporations, 81
Striking committees, 32
Subamendments, 23, 26, 48-49, 99-100
Subcommittees, 61
Supplementary questions, 30
Supply bills, 16, 31, 34, 35
Suspension: of members, 20, 29-30; of rules, 40, 95
Synods, 40

Tabling, 17, 51
Table Officer, 27
Tax bills, 17, 34
Tellers, 17, 66, 74, 78; *see also* Scrutineers
Tie-breaking procedures, 75
Trespass, 64-65
Trust companies, 82
Two-thirds vote, 17

Unanimous shareholders' agreement, 92, 93
Unanimous votes, 75
Unfinished business, 87, 88
Unlawful assemblies, 64-65
Unparliamentary language, 17, 20

Voting, 27, 66; at shareholders' meetings, 91; for a political candidate, 77-79; in Parliament, 27; methods of, 54-55; shares, 88; recording, 93; *see also* Ballot, Casting vote

Warden, 42
Ways and means bills, 17, 34